"I AM THAT I AM"

THE SELF-REVEALING LIGHT

THE I-AM-SELF

REALITIES SUPERNAL

"I AM THAT I AM"

THE SELF-REVEALING LIGHT

THE I-AM-SELF

REALITIES SUPERNAL

Lillian DeWaters

*"And God said unto Moses,
I Am That I Am."*

"I AM THAT I AM"

First Mystics of the World Edition 2014
Published by Mystics of the World

ISBN-13: 978-0692235959
ISBN-10: 0692235957
Title ID: 4847158

For information contact:
Mystics of the World
Eliot, Maine
www.mysticsoftheworld.com

Cover graphics by Margra Muirhead
Printed by CreateSpace
Available from Mystics of the World and Amazon.com

DeWaters, Lillian, 1883 – 1964
Originally published:
Lillian DeWaters Publications
Stamford, Connecticut, 1938

CONTENTS

PREFACE

EVER since I can remember I have been deeply interested in life and spiritual things. Since early girlhood I have ever been seeking more light, and am always the happiest when some definite revelation is given me.

Since the very beginning of my writing in 1908, each one of my books has been a chapter out of my own life's experience. No matter how happily and contentedly I may have basked in the experience of the one eternal day, soon I would find myself again hungering and thirsting for more of the same real substance, and so would again take up the search for more light.

To me, progress in spiritual light and revelation is absolutely essential to joyous, healthy, active experience. I always long to freshly feed on manna from on high, new and vivifying. This provides me with inspiration, enthusiasm, ardor, love, peace, and contentment. Many times I have seen people apparently content to think and live, as it were, entirely confined to certain prescribed teachers, books, and writings, and I have often wondered why they should so deprive themselves of the unparalleled glory of Self-revelation.

Unless we seek direct contact with God by way of our own heart and inner feeling, how shall divine prophecy ever come to pass—"And they shall all be taught of God"? The revelation of God to man, you can surely see, and must admit, could not have come to a close, since God is infinite and so must infinitely reveal Himself to us. No certain revelation could ever be a final one inasmuch as there is no end to God.

Dear friends, the time is here, for everyone to remove from himself all mental restrictions, for they only cramp and limit one's growth in Truth and so prevent the much desired individual revelation and unfoldment. Life and Its ever-revealing ideas and realities await to bless us all; thus we should not remain satisfied with the measure of light and progress we may have, but ever be alive to the deeper and more glorious realities waiting just ahead of us. Such inner, joyous and happy aspirations after "the deep things of God" (which will become the very practical things we now stand in need of) keep us always in a delightful, active and animated state, and bring us a rich reward.

So be assured that you may now place yourself in touch with direct divine illumination and revelation as set forth in this series, and in gaining such illumination you will likewise partake of happiness such as you have never before experienced.

In the early days of my study in Truth, within me were two most important questions for which I never received permanently satisfying answers. They were these: Where and how did evil begin? How is it that I consider myself a Son of God and feel that I represent the spiritual, perfect man, still I walk about in a physical form and live, apparently, in a material world of strife? Then another very puzzling question to me was this: Who or what are the "mortals" mentioned so frequently in certain truth literature?

My search for answers to these perplexing questions never altogether ceased until about two years ago when one day, while not thinking at all along these lines, suddenly I was enveloped in a bright light and certain distinct revelation was given me relative to the origin of evil. Greatly astonished, amazed, and even at first bewildered, I listened, for the answer coincided with nothing that I had previously been taught. This revelation proved to be the first of many others which have since followed.

As a result of this first light, I wrote and published my book, *The Price of Glory*, which has been so happily received by many. After this, much more light was revealed to me, and then one never-to-be-forgotten day, I received the answer to that long-asked question: Who are the mortals? This answer straightened out many other things for me, and often in a way diametrically different to what I had ever suspected.

In writing this "I AM THAT I AM" Series, I am constrained to say that I feel certain such revelations have come to me only because I have been willing to share with the world such precious moments. I feel confident that we all should do even as Paul admonished: "As every man hath received the gift, even so minister the same, one to another." Jesus, too, definitely stated, "Give, and it shall be given unto you." So we must be willing to surrender all that is required of us in order to lovingly obey Jesus' thrice repeated admonition, "Feed my sheep."

Within the pages of this series I have presented the origin of evil as given me by the Self-revealing Light. I recall now how at one time in my life I accepted the idea that evil had no origin; in fact, that such were impossible, since if one were to find the answer to it, he would be giving reality to that which is unreal, and so making evil a fact. Now, strangely enough, the exact opposite of this view is the logical one, as I will show you in a very simple way. Truth has no origin, that is, Truth is without beginning or end. Had evil no origin in belief, it would be as eternal as Truth. Is this not so? But as we find it easy to believe that evil will someday come to an end, even as the Bible tells, then it must have had a beginning, for nothing can end unless it began. Furthermore, to locate the source of evil and destroy it, *there* is the only way to bring its history to a close and so make way for the millennium.

Thus the mistaken belief that evil has no beginning must now give place to the contrary new idea and so help bring its so-called reign to a close. All who are living in the light will surely welcome the radiant glory of the dawning day. It is wise to give no undue attention to the personal channel through which any revelation comes, that you may enjoy to the utmost the radiance of the light, and glorify the Christ-Self which sheds it.

During this past summer fuller illumination regarding many things came to me. For instance, in this series I present the light which was revealed to me on the following subjects: Jesus Christ; Love-Wisdom; the Self-revealing Light; the I-Am-Self; demonstrating supply, or multiplying our good; the original sin; our real and unreal states; male and female; the Adam dream; marriage and happiness; the seven days; and many other subjects.

Thus may the Love-Light revealed and diffused within these pages be the "quickening Spirit" which will arouse all who read them to recognize their own Christ-Self as able and willing to impart direct divine illumination and revelation to them, thus being the Self-revealing Light in whose light "shall we see light."

As the light found herein has been given the author in response to her constant reaching out for it, and her willingness to share it with others, so may each one of you be so illumined, exalted, and established in this absolute truth that you, too, will gladly spread it and share it with others. For "he that hath" access to the Self-revealing Light, "to him shall be given" a continuous revelation of that light, until the darkness has completely vanished from sight and there is one eternal day.

—Lillian DeWaters

THE SELF-REVEALING LIGHT

I come to tell you the truth of the perfect, original man and the perfect original universe. I come to show you how you may experience health and harmony, here and now, by the apprehension and understanding that you, yourself, in very truth, are the way to these by following the Self-revealing Light.

In Jesus' parable, the prodigal son was not required to make over or repair "a far country" so that he might live there in peace and happiness. Nor did he begin to destroy any evil there. All that was needful in order to experience peace, harmony and abundant good, was for him to leave that far country and return to the truth of his own Being.

Now "a far country" was never intended to mean a *place*. It is *a state of belief* which man experiences when he loses sight of himself and his perfection as in and of the Christ who is eternally one with the Father—the I AM THAT I AM. Choosing to leave the conscious awareness of spiritually possessing all that the Father hath, man became what Jesus termed, "a prodigal son."

As we apprehend what constitutes such a false state of belief and turn from it to the truth, we shall each be fulfilling the prophecy implied in Jesus' parable: for the return of the prodigal to the Father's house of perfection surely refers to none other than ourselves.

The conscious awareness of this perfection, and its ever accompanying experience, was the *original* state of man in his Father's house. Knowing his oneness and inseparableness with the Father, and all that this relationship includes, and functioning herein, man is ever the Son of God in his original, pristine state. In the parable, this true position of man is portrayed by the rich man's son in his father's house *before* he desired to personalize his possessions and go into a far country.

Inasmuch as no one could ever be separated from himself, none of us has ever been separated from the Christ-Self, for we have his promise, "Lo, I am with you always." Likewise, we can never be alienated from God, our Father, since ever Father and Son are one whole and inseparable reality or Being.

The belief in the common illusion that we are alienated from our Father's house, from God, our Father-Mother, is a deception. *It is not true!* Father and Son are ever *one*, and such relation can never be severed.

14

When we rise in vision and in the perception of the truth of things as they are, we see that we are eternally one with the Father, *through the Son,* hence, eternally in the Father's house, never having departed from it. Any contrary beliefs are like dreams or mistakes—no truth abiding in them.

Really, we have never lived outside the kingdom of heaven. When we actually perceive this to *be* so, our whole outlook changes from a state of mortal seeing to the viewpoint of the redeemed state of awareness. For illustration, suppose that while a man sleeps at home, he dreams that he is a thousand miles away. How shall he be brought back? How shall he travel those thousand miles so as to be in his own home again?

One might answer, "Let him awake." But would this bring him back? Obviously, no, since he never left home. There is no way that he could come back, for how could he return to a place from which he never went away? An awakening, however, would restore him to the conscious experience of what was really so.

Similarly, we cannot use and enjoy our heavenly good so long as we assume that we have left it! Or so long as we look for a way or a method to transplant us from one place to another or from one being to another.

Then why, one may ask, did Jesus infer that the prodigal should return home? The answer is: Man must re-turn, or turn within to his eternal home—the *truth of his own Being*—to that which has never changed, and is so *now*. Man must perceive that he *never* left his Father's house; *never* wandered away; *never* was lost in a dream, for this were impossible!

Any contrary thinking is no thinking at all. One need not attempt to destroy or change things which happen in a dream. This is not the point of clear vision. He must see that if the kingdom of heaven is within him, and all about him, as Jesus said, then he is ever in that kingdom, and there now.

The belief that he is connected or associated with a state wherein he fell a victim to sickness, sin, and all kinds of limitation, is *a false* belief which must be refuted and erased from him. He must turn to that state of knowing which is no part of a dream—not return as though he were retracing his steps, but only as though he were letting go of the belief that he had ever left the perfect state.

Then the very things which seem discordant and distressing will fade away, and in their place will appear forms of experience as they really are. Nor need we move from where we are in order that this stupendous fact take hold of us and this glorifying transfiguration take place. For, "The place whereon thou standest is holy ground."

Unless one clearly perceives the nothingness of belief in what is *not so*, with all its fantastic imaginations, he is like the fly caught in the web, that is, while he so dreams, he believes it is a reality. Jesus showed us that even should one believe himself a prodigal son, he may release himself from this false state by identifying himself with the consciousness of the Father, which is the I AM THAT I AM, and may then say with Jesus, "All things that the Father hath are mine."

In turning to the spiritual state of life and things, by placing himself in the Son-Self position, man simultaneously identifies himself with God, his real Being, *in whom no evil can possibly dwell:* for it is only because he believes that he has separated himself from this true state that he entertains the sense of being alienated from the Father's house.

Placing himself in his true position and functioning here in thought and feeling, Lo! he has found himself, or has returned to his true estate. Here he knows his real identity and joyously declares, *"I am the light of the world! I am the living bread! I am he that liveth, and behold, I am alive for evermore! He that hath seen me hath seen the Father!"*

"I will arise in realization and go to my Father by way of my own true Self," exultingly cries the prodigal when becoming aware of the truth of his Being. "I will leave the belief that I have separated

myself from my true state and my eternal inheritance, and must find my way back to it through
labor and strife. I will leave the belief that I am
wretched in mind and body, weary of living,
deprived of good—and I will take the position of
being *now* in my Father's house and as never
having been alienated from it. Here my spiritual
sense assures me of peace and glory, joy and
gladness, and I see profusion and abundance
everywhere."

Reader, are *you* ready to dismiss the thought
of having left the house of abundant good? Are
you ready to leave sickness, for instance, without
attempting in some way to destroy it? Remember
Jesus' words: "I am not come to destroy, but to
fulfill." We all, as the prodigal, have believed that
we left the kingdom of love and harmony: but we
all must dismiss this belief if we would come into
our inheritance.

Roll away the stone of mistaken thinking, and
may there come forth in you that mind which is
Love—"that mind which was also in Christ Jesus."
See with the eyes of Love, feel with the heart of
Love: for *"Love never faileth."* Love is the light-
beam of the sun of righteousness on which comes
the glad recognition of "Christ in you, the hope of
glory." Turning from a false sense of mind and its
thinking to Love and Its feeling, one soon finds the
way out of a far country. Love, seeing perfection
only, sees nothing to forgive, nothing to be

destroyed. Love meets the prodigal with a kiss. Love prepares a feast of good things. Love rejoices and is exceedingly glad. Love is satisfied just to be Love—the forever I AM.

The Love which is also Wisdom is not subservient to this or that accepted dogma, to this or that material trend of things. For Love-Wisdom is the fulfilling of the law; Its own health; Its own wealth; Its own happiness; Its own peace. Love-Wisdom is the Self-existent, the Self-sufficient— the Self-revealing I AM.

The great point to be considered by you is this: Are you embracing the idea of your spiritual reality, or are you identifying yourself with a material existence? With God or with man? With inspirational or with human thinking? With the one divine Mind, or are you conceding a separate human mind as well?

Man, having assumed that he long ago left his Father's house, associates himself in imagination with pairs of opposites—good and evil, life and death, and limitations of time and place. His wealth and success, too, depend largely upon his attitude toward people, circumstances, time and conditions. But he can *never* find complete peace there, simply because complete peace is not found in false estimates.

When man identifies himself with Spirit, with the one Mind, he sees that he can no longer believe in another mind as he once did. In the Self-

19

revealing Light he sees the I AM THAT I AM and knows his inherent oneness with It, so does not attempt to cultivate or spiritualize a human mind, believing by this method to arrive at that mind which was in Christ Jesus. Neither does he attempt to heal or change a body which he considers material, in order to bring it into the real state of health and harmony.

Many, no doubt, have been greatly helped, apparently, by making use of a mental method of healing, but the moment arrives for each and every one of us when we must advance beyond the method of merely changing the things in a dream world.

Our perception and thought may change, but our real state, which the perfect Christ-Self embodies, ever remains the same—"That was the true light which lighteth every man that cometh into the world" (John 1:9). The Light-Man is unaffected by any and all of the various reasons, emotions, conditions and circumstances of a dream. Irrefutably, in the one Christ state rests our supply of every good thing and thought.

But if we suppose that we may place our health in a personal body or in a personal mind, we are as in a dream; and only when we see that our health, our wealth, and our happiness, as well as our supply of every good, exists *already* in the Son-Self, ever one with God, do we come face to face with our perfection and reality, and so we cease to labor and to strive.

There is a path which offers deliverance from every ill. It is mystically described in Jesus' words: "I am the way; I am the light; I am the resurrection." *One is himself the radiant Light:* but not until he perceives that already, in his real state, he is the Son-Self who is always one with the Father, does he apprehend the luminous meaning in those mystical words—"I am the way."

This *I* does not refer to Jesus as a personal man, nor to Jesus even as the best man who ever lived among us. This *I* means *the Christ,* the Son operating in the state of perfection—that state of conscious, perfect knowing, feeling, and experiencing, which is ever one with the Father. This Christ state not only inhered in Jesus but also inheres in every one of us, now and always, as the hidden, inner man of the heart.

Verily, it is this Christ state, it is this inner man of the heart, who is our way—*the way*—out of a dream-belief into reality; out of a far country into the Father's house; and out of a false state of identity into being the Christ-Man, and no other.

Jesus was the "wayshower" only insomuch as he exemplified the way to us who have believed we are in a far country. Functioning in the position of the Christ, he spoke as *He* when he declared, "I am the way." It is the *I*, said he, the Self, or the Son of God in his real and true position of conscious

21

awareness and expression, who states: I am the way for you out of a false state, since it is only by unifying yourselves with your own true Selfhood that you can find your way into your true home and say with me, "I and my Father are one."

Truly, none of us will ever become conscious of, and alive to, our relation to the Father except through Jesus Christ as the way, for he alone illustrated to us the original perfect man, the embodied Christ state. Thus he, as the Christ-Self, is the only way out of a self-imposed state of false belief and misconception.

"I am the door. He that entereth not by the door into the sheepfold, but climbeth up some other way, the same is a thief and a robber. By me if any man enter in, he shall be saved, and shall go in and out, and find pasture" (John 10:1-9).

Should one seek to resume the conscious awareness of his true relation with the Father in some other way than by accepting and embodying the original Christ state as ever-existent, and thus as the only way of redemption for us all, he will not be truly preparing himself for the reinstatement in his Father's house, nor be fathoming Jesus' words, "I am the door."

I, your very Christ-Self, am the door. If the Son— your real Son-Self—shall make you free, ye shall be free indeed. Without Me, your Self functioning in your true position, ye can do nothing. Behold,

I—your original, ever-existing Perfection—make all things new.

It is quite generally believed that the only way one can think is by the use of a human mind, and that by spiritualizing it he may use it to think divinely. Yet the perfect Mind already exists—and exists within us now, that is, it is *our* mind. Now, "a house divided against itself cannot stand," and to claim that a human mind is responsible for all evil, yet that by thinking good thoughts with it, it may be spiritualized or transformed into the mind of Christ, surely indicates a divided kingdom—a fountain sending forth both sweet water and bitter.

The fact is, man may think divinely without heeding in any way a so-called human mind. As he identifies himself with the one divine Mind, which belongs to him as the Son of God, he will begin to think and feel intuitively and inspiration-ally. Such thoughts and emotions spring from the Christ-Self which is ever one with the Father. This divine thinking is accompanied by light, peace, harmony and power. Then one's affairs will also express the wondrous peace and harmony of this Self-revealing Light.

All inspiration and intuition result in loving feeling; these are not to be lightly rated, but are indeed the divine realities in life, by which, effortlessly, we recognize that we are in the kingdom where there is no need to labor, for love and light make existence an ever-joyous experience. So, instead of forcing yourself to mechanically repeat certain thoughts or statements of truth, begin now *to feel* after God with all your heart and so you shall find Him, and find as well all that is beautiful and true.

"They should seek the Lord, if haply they might feel after him, and find him, though he be not far from every one of us" (Acts 17:27).

Love and Mind should be seen to be an identical source, united in action as one, not two. The result is thought warmed by love, and love guided by wisdom. That love, felt in the heart, is the Love which is our true Selfhood. Therefore, do not struggle to reason out the things of Spirit, for they can best make themselves known through the heart. If you read a book, for instance, which human reason has penned, then only human reason will understand it. But if the Mind of Love conceived the ideas, then it will take the Mind of Love to be able to comprehend them.

If a certain book does not promote light and love in you, either you have not prepared yourself for its blessing, or the book lacks that blessing. Certain it is that only those books which disclose the I-Am-Self within each and every one of us, can shed the Self-revealing Light.

It is only to the degree that we *love*, that the Mind of light and understanding is revealed to us. And love will also be the means of acquainting us with the *body* of light. Jesus, on the mount, presented his body changed from the usual human appearance to that of such brilliant light that it blinded the eyes of the three disciples with him. This is the true body: our real light-body, no less than his. It has outline as well as colors of imperishable beauty and loveliness.

No matter what you may call yourself or think that you may be, your real Christ state remains ever the same. It is unalterable — "the same yesterday, today, and forever." Remember, the prodigal in Jesus' parable was still the rich man's son. Nothing, not even his belief in poverty, hunger, and squalor could ever change his true identity; nor can anything change yours.

Man, by not giving himself up to the objective of his real mind, heart and body (which truly comprise his identity), believing that he is but mortal and material, is in a state of false supposition. He is far from the discernment that there is but one all-inclusive Christ-Mind, one all-inclusive Christ-Self, and one all-inclusive Christ-Body. He has wandered away from the true idea of Reality and his eternal oneness with It; instead, he believes that he is of human origin, so many years of age and living in some city in a material world of strife. No wonder that Jesus called this state of belief, "a far country"!

Our identity is one, not two! When this misconception of two men, the immortal and the mortal, is cleared away, then will teachers and students cease identifying themselves with mortals and hasten to claim their true estate as that of the immortal, here and now—even in a so-called physical world.

Claiming that there is but one man, who is spiritual and immortal always, and that inherently we are he, and yet continually contending with another man, called a "mortal," has resulted in a confused state of thought, since one does not see clearly how he can actually be the spiritual perfect man and yet function in a physical, mortal state; nor what relationship, if any, he bears to a so-called mortal man.

There is a simple way out of this dilemma, which has been disclosed by the Self-revealing Light. It is to stand *definitely* upon the platform that there is, and ever has been, but one man— God's man—and never swerve from this position.

Next, see that while this one man can never change his identity nor sever his relationship with the Father, he may, however, (as illustrated in Jesus' parable and, obviously, in our own lives) operate in different states of awareness. His true state, or the state in which he functioned originally and which state ever exists in him, even here and now, is called *the Christ*. Operating here, as Jesus exemplified to us in his own life, he is the Christ-Man, the immortal Son of God.

When it is clearly seen that the immortal and a mortal are not two men but *two states of the same man*—one the real and the other the unreal—then the great confusion and the consequent misstatements regarding the immortal man and a mortal man will vanish, and with them will go other misconceptions as well, for the Self-revealing Light is indeed far reaching.

Always the Christ state abides in man, and when he functions here he is verily the Christ-Man and no other, even as Jesus was, and still is. Should man choose to desire to take his possessions and leave his Father's house (as related in the parable) inevitably he would wander (in belief) into another state, called a mortal state, to be more or less unconscious or unaware of the real truth of his being: and here in this false and unreal state, he is wrongly termed a mortal man.

As we all know, in very truth, no state of sleep or dream ever changes one man into another, nor makes him two selves instead of one, as he really is. Though he may change from one *state* to another, though he may leave, apparently, one state for another, still he is ever the same man.

Mind is one, not two! When the notion that there are two minds, one the divine and the other a personal mentality, is seen to be a superficial misconception, since the God-Mind is the only mind there is or ever could be—then man will be set free from a false belief that he has a human mind which he is expected, somehow, to change into the mind of Christ.

Man, in his true Christ position, uses the one and only God-Mind: when he wandered from his true position, he simultaneously left the awareness of this mind as being his, always, and in this ignorant or false state he called his mind "human."

To say or to declare that there is but one Mind, that is, God, and still think and speak of *another*, brings perplexity and confusion into the thought of the seeker: but to see and be alive to the fact that the one Mind is the real and only, while the "other" is but self-imposed, hence unreal and non-existent, frees one from misconception and its consequent misinterpretation.

The light of the Self enables us not only to see clearly the things as they are, but likewise empowers us to speak about them in a correct and lucid manner.

Body is one, not two! There will never be more than one body—the body of God. Your belief that your body is material in substance, hence mortal and subject to pain, disease, and death, must some day yield to the truth of Being, which is that man never has a personal body for which he is responsible: for the true light-body is always spiritual and perfect, since ever one with the perfect creation.

Man, functioning in his true or Christ state of mind, expresses no other than the body of Christ.

For how could it be otherwise? Verily his face shines "as the sun" and his raiment is "white as the light," even as Jesus manifested on the mount of transfiguration.

So it is that the notion of dual men, dual minds, and dual bodies must be seen to be altogether false and erroneous, and absolutely contrary to the fact that there is but one Mind, one Christ and one Body. This is the One in the all, and all in One.

Now, the term "the real man," which we often hear expressed among us, simply means yourself as you *really* are. There are never two selves of you, one the spiritual and the other a mortal. You are always one entity — God's man. You never have two minds, one the Divine and the other a human mentality, nor do you ever have two bodies, one spiritual and perfect and the other material and imperfect. You may, however, even as God's man (whom you know you are) entertain false beliefs. Is this not so?

Ever our identity is the same in sickness as in health, in death as in life, in a so-called physical world as in the real, spiritual universe. Therefore we should recognize ourselves as immortals here and now, notwithstanding human beliefs and appearances to the contrary.

In our real state of awareness and manifestation we are the real man who knows himself to be one with God. Only when we believe ourselves otherwise do we find a state where sin, sickness, and death appear and then call ourselves "poor mortals."

Take as a helpful illustration, the simple fact that two and two are four. Is not this fact in every place and at any time? Is it true that two and two could be five in a false belief or in a dream? You may answer, "Yes, two and two might then be five in a dream or in a false belief, but of course, not in reality." Then you would be mistaken, for two and two could never be other than four, though they might seem so to you while dreaming. Anywhere, even in a dream or a delusion, two and two could not be other than four.

In the same way, man is ever one with Christ and Christ is ever one with God. Always, in heaven and earth, in a dream of a material existence, and even in the experience called death, such relationship exists and abides. To actively perceive and accept this verity is to be set free from the opposite false belief and its distorted experiences.

"Look unto me and be ye saved, all the ends of the earth," says the Christ in you. Remove your eyes from a sick-appearing body and place your vision on Me, your real Self, the Alpha and Omega of your action, feeling and form. *I* am your Self in the finished kingdom, and *I* am still your Self in the seemingly material world. *I* fill all space; *I* manifest harmony and perfection wherever *I* am —

and *I* am everywhere. Do not, therefore, limit Me, your real Self, to some world or plane beyond where you now stand, but *right here I* am your mind, *I* am your body, and *I* am the light of your world.

Jesus Christ, the messenger from on high, overcame death and the grave through the conscious knowledge of his eternal oneness with the Father: and "Jesus Christ" is the real "family name" for us all. Though we have called ourselves children of men, human beings, mortals—in the Self-revealing Light we see ourselves as immortals, children of the Light, the same as he. Indeed this is the real man, "who is the image of the invisible God, the firstborn of every creature."

Jesus never believed himself to be a mortal man as we have done. He was an immortal who was aware of his immortal nature. He knew that he and the Father were one and identical. He spoke and acted from his God-Being. He knew that he was the life, the truth and the way, and he said so, for he knew that the one Life includes all life, and the one Being includes all being.

He knew that man had lost sight of his oneness with the Christ-Self, hence his consequent failures in any adventures outside the conscious awareness of his completeness and perfection as ever Self-existent. This is why the parable states: "This, My Son was dead" —(*believing* himself separated from Me), "and is alive again" —(recognizing

31

his error). "He was lost" (in the former belief) "and is found" (in the latter understanding).

The spiritual fact that man is one, and this one is the Christ-Man, should not be taken merely as a statement of truth while one continues to think and live in the same, ordinary manner as before, thinking and speaking of a mortal man, a human mind, and a material body. You should perceive this stupendous fact with such arresting and never-to-be-forgotten insight and discernment that from this instant you become a new creature. You will begin right now to identify yourself with the *real* man, despite any seeming mortal belief or appearance to the contrary.

Why locate the real man as off in space somewhere? Or why think of him as in some state other than where you now find yourself to be? Why not see and understand at once, and for all time to come, that there are never two of you—one in the spiritual universe and the other in a material world, anymore than there are two of you if you sleep and dream that you are swimming in the ocean. You can readily see that there are not two of you then, one on the bed and the other in the water. All the while there is but one man, or identity, though he may be in two states—the waking and sleeping states, one real and true, the other unreal and untrue.

Now, regardless of what you think or feel yourself to be, you are ever the selfsame man; nor could any dream of life separate you in any way from your Self.

When this fact is actually and vividly perceived to be so, students of truth will cease to separate man in two parts; moreover, they will cease thinking and teaching after this fashion. Instead, they will see that what are *thought* to be two entities are two states of man — one the actual, and the other the seeming.

Man may be in varying and different degrees of awareness, but nothing can change the fact that he is God's man just the same. This is unalterably true, from everlasting to everlasting. And should he find himself in a dream, involving a false belief of limitation or trouble of any kind, even *there* he may prove himself to be the real man, God's man intact, by consciously exercising his birthright and asserting that there is ever but the one Mind, one Christ-Man and one experience.

It was *while* Jesus walked on earth in the form of the son of man, or as an ordinary human being, that he made the claim, "I and my Father are one." It was among the great throngs of people that the voice from heaven was heard, saying, "This is My beloved Son." And where men brought in to him a man sick of the palsy, at Jesus' command he arose, whole.

If God's real man had not been there, right where he who was sick of the palsy appeared to be, how then could such a transformation have taken place? Beyond any doubt, whenever and wherever Jesus performed his miracles, then and at that place he saw the selfsame man eternally at-one with the Father—even when he raised to life his friend Lazarus, who appeared to be dead.

Man in his true state is the only real man there is. And he now exists right where you are, for how could he be "closer than breathing, nearer than hands and feet" were this not so, and were he not *your Self?* Can you not see that it is only because you are seeing and thinking of man as two beings, one in the spiritual state and the other in the mortal state, that you limit your vision and thus circumscribe your experience of health, harmony, and happiness?

As soon as you actually perceive that the real man is the man you should now acknowledge yourself to be—and no other—then you will begin to lose the false sense (dream) of yourself as being otherwise; and you will also cease to believe that the perfect man is distant from where you find yourself to be *right* now.

"If I make my bed in hell, behold, thou art there." Even though I think of myself as in the depths of despair, limitation and bondage, even there Thou, my Self, art with me. The darkness of false beliefs and their dream shadows cannot hide this luminous understanding from me.

"It is I, be not afraid," explained the all-under-standing Jesus. *It is I!* It is the self-same *I*, the one I

AM. It is not I as man separated from him-Self and other selves, but it is *I*, the universal Christ-Self. "Lo, *I* am with you alway." *I* am you, and you are (the one) *I*. There is no other.

And it is *I* who come to you now. Will you listen to My voice calling you away from that false state of believing? You will never be able to find happiness, harmony and prosperity in a false dependence apart from Me, your own Selfhood. Your heart's desire can never be fulfilled outside of the knowledge that *I* am your Being of completeness and fulfillment, always. *I* am your world of success and abundance here, there, everywhere.

You are not subject to a foolish mind and its thinking. You are not bound by a frail body and its feelings. You are not led astray by wrong thoughts and resultant reasonings. These are but dreams — the things you think and feel in your *supposed* departure from Me. Recognize that you never really left Me, and soon you will lose your dream of separateness, share in the awareness of reality, and participate in the experience of wholeness and abundance.

I am the still, small Voice which speaks to you. *I* am the radiant path of light which is inviting you. *I* am the "everlasting arms" which embrace and hold you. "Lo, I will never leave you nor forsake you," for *I* am You, your-Self.

"My grace is sufficient for you." Turn away from the imperfect man-made laws on a so-called physical plane; turn away also from the imperfect man-made laws on a so-called metaphysical plane. Take the freedom which *I* give unto you. Be My law of perpetual good unto yourself. Believe no longer in physical or mental cause and effect, for listen carefully to My question, "Who did sin, this man or his parents?" And my answer, "Neither hath this man sinned nor his parents: but that the works of God should be made manifest in him." And again, *I* ask, "Which of you convinceth me of sin?"

Behold, to Me the darkness and the light of human experience are the same, for *I* see nothing but Myself and My own radiant glory. Thou, too, art of the heavenly world of light and glory, and every one of you is now and always in and of Me, and *I* am ever in the Father's house of harmony, love and abundance. *"Believest thou this?"*

I AM! Therefore I am not dependent upon people, places or things for my happiness or prosperity, since, as the real man, I am ever one with the I AM THAT I AM which is Self-existent—depending upon nothing but Itself. By recognizing this truth of Being and not looking elsewhere for my good, or seeking for it outside the one Selfhood, automatically I find my Self and my abundance of all-good right at hand, as one with the I AM THAT I AM and never separated from It. Thus I am redeemed from the false belief of personality and separation, and restored to the state of the real man—my Self, as I really am

I AM! As the real man, my health originates in and is dependent upon nothing but my conscious awareness of my oneness with the I AM THAT I AM. Health and wholeness are not located in any kind of body, but *only* in God, the Creator of all. Locating my health or harmony here, I know that it is present and that it is perfect; it is indestructible and constant. I therefore dismiss the false belief that health depends upon bodily states or conditions, or upon personal mental states and thoughts. I perceive that health is wholeness, unlimited and unconditioned always, and that in proportion as I see and accept myself as ever I AM, free and impersonal, dependent upon nothing but that which *is*, I have the glorious experience of that light of Christ "which lighteth every man that cometh into the world."

I AM! My peace, harmony and happiness can never actually be interrupted or impaired in any way, because depending wholly upon my conscious awareness of my Self as I AM. Thus, I rejoice with exceeding great joy in finding myself at home and in my Father's house.

"And when he came to himself, he said, I will arise and go to my Father." *When he came to himself!* When he saw himself as he really was. When he became consciously aware of his identity as the Son of God ever one with the Father, then he cried: I will return to my Self, to my own I AM, and to the one Consciousness which made all and includes all.

The belief that erring thinking is a reality and that it has power to interfere with the harmony of man's being is a form of sin. Such thinking should be recognized as *unreal* because not originating in the one God-Mind. When this recognition comes, it is because the true spiritual sense is present to bear witness that "the accuser of our brethren is cast down, which accused them before our God, day and night."

Who invented the laws of physical or mental cause and effect? Who invented the law of sin and death? "God hath made man upright; but *they* have sought out many inventions." So man, *believing* that he could find joy and happiness outside of himself, finds deprivation and despair; for saith the Christ-Self, "If therefore the light that is in thee be darkness, how great is that darkness!"

When the Self-revealing Light enveloped Daniel, it became perfectly safe for him to encounter any danger, and he remained with the lions, unharmed. Nor was "the cup" removed from Jesus, in order that he might prove life to be deathless and triumphant. It was the same Self-revealing Light which transformed that shameful hour into sublime glory.

Only because we had a desire to look outside the Father's house for our good, did we feel a sense of separation from Him, our perfect Being, and did we begin calling ourselves independent thinkers, with personal human minds and personal physical bodies. *But none of it is true!* And by recognizing and experiencing this in the Self-revealing Light, we may likewise partake of Its transcendent power to help and heal.

Disbelief in any sense of separation will awake and thus aid us in the full restoration to our pristine state of awareness—the conscious knowledge and glory of the completeness of our good in the Father's house—the I AM THAT I AM.

So, dear reader, give all your consideration and loving will to the possession of the one Mind, and the one Mind only. Why speak or think or write adversely about another if you are able to accept and claim there is but the One? Cannot you see that the very fact that an individual thus speaks of another shows that *to him* there is another mind?

Who told you that you had a mind of your own? Certainly not God. Therefore, instead of calling your mind a "mentality" and considering it the seat of either wrong beliefs or right thinking, let go of the mistaken thought of it altogether!

The one, infinite I-Am-Mind is now and ever sufficient for every one of us. How could there be an infinite, illimitable God-Mind and still millions of other human minds or mentalities? When one beholds this stupendous revelation, as unfolded by the Self-revealing Light, it will indeed seem strange to him that he could ever have believed otherwise.

Determine, therefore, to so fully accept and feel that it is the one divine Mind with which you are thinking and knowing, that you will quickly free yourself from the wrong viewpoint. You will then be liberated from the erring belief that you should make changes and renovations in a human mind and from ever thinking or speaking about some personal human-thinking organ or instrument.

Place your vision and all your feeling so trustingly and absolutely in the truth that the one God-Mind is the only Mind there is, or ever could be, infinite in understanding, wisdom and light, that you feel the enriching satisfaction which comes from this liberating viewpoint. When you thus identify yourself with the Father-God through the Son, or Christ-Self, you will simultaneously be freeing yourself from discordant, limited results produced by your former lack of discernment.

Also, dear reader, see the larger and fuller truth about your body. When do you expect to come into possession of the real body of light in place of an appearance of materiality which is mortal? Surely not before you plainly see, and intelligently understand, the true body to be ever included in the Christ-Body, and hence, as present always.

In a dream, one sees the effects of dreaming; so in false believing one sees the results of it in myriads of discordant and limited things and situations about him. But as he wakens, or becomes alive to his true state, he loses that distorted outlook and feeling and comes definitely in touch with the reality of all things.

Always when one is willing to acknowledge his mistake and to repent of it, then he is ready for the blessing. He soon learns that this previous distortion misinterpreted all things and that a clearer vision of his inseparability from that Self which is ever one with God, together with a loving, willing heart, reports things to him as they rightly are.

Now, as far as the body is concerned, see the one Body as ever one with the God-Mind—that Mind which is yours eternally; and as with a false belief in a separate self you saw and felt a personal, limited body, so now possessing sovereign power to think rightly and knowing your Self to be one with the universal Christ, you will naturally see and feel a body which expresses wholeness and harmony.

Then you will joyously make your claim with the apostle Paul, "What? Know ye not that your body is the temple of the Holy Ghost which is in you, which ye have of God?" Moreover you will cease to call it mortal or human, nor longer believe it physical or limited.

In the Self-revealing Light you can see none other than that God is Spirit, and Spirit is *all*, and so all is "very good." You can now understand why the one Mind is represented by an infinite creation of expression, and why the latter *must be*—and can logically be seen to be the body of God.

Your body and my body therefore could *never* be personal or physical, any more than the figure five is personal or physical. We all share this figure equally, and it would be impossible to personalize it. It is the same with the one Christ-Body—the body which expresses the one Christ state. It is not ours personally, but it is ours impersonally. We see that my body is not your body nor vice versa, but we each possess an individualized expression of the one Christ-Body, just as we may share in possessing and comprehending the one Christ-Mind.

When we discard the *mis*conception of body and begin thinking of it as one with Love, one with Life eternal, when we see it as the perfect creation, then of course, the form of imperfection which we now see will fade from view, to be replaced by form in its true relation to the Creator. Thus shall all false creation be transfigured until we see as God sees and know that we walk in the finished kingdom where beauty, love, and harmony abide and abound.

In the degree that we are able to become released from the personal belief that we may have of ourselves as independent thinkers and doers, becoming more and more aware of and at-one with our true Christ-Self which is ever one with the God-Consciousness, we are *automatically* lifted out of a dream of personality into a more perfect experience of reality and harmony. Then our full deliverance from personal sense and dream shall have been accomplished.

Therefore, if one is entertaining a sense of sickness, of discord or of limitation, let him first of all know that it is only a personal sense of life and things; it is not the Christ-Consciousness, and because such a false sense is unreal, it may obviously be dispelled. Such a false sense of life is in and of the dream we entertain that we are detached from our real Self, while the fact is that no dream could ever part us.

As we release ourselves from the belief that we have a human mind or mentality, which thinks good and evil, and a body of flesh and blood which we are expected, somehow, to personally supervise and control, we shall be turning toward our true Selfhood and taking the first steps toward our reinstatement in our Father's house.

Since the Christ state of man remains unchangeable, "the same yesterday, today, and forever," then all my happiness and harmony are intact and actively present always, *awaiting only my conscious awareness to set me free from a dream.* Finding my All-in-all as ever in the Christ-Selfhood and never absent from It (since the Son is always one with the Father) I awake, as it were, in the kingdom of heaven to find that I have never left it, and that any dream to the contrary temporarily may have veiled but never actually intercepted my vision— "which veil is done away (as I function) in the Christ."

Let us recognize and accept with joy the perfect Selfhood—the I AM—which is so, not because of anything we personally say or think or do, but only because It is ever one with the I AM THAT I AM. Then it is that we gladly, rejoicingly, leave a far country and its false gods, to obey the first commandment and worship the one God in spirit and in truth.

Since God is Life, and there is but one God, there is and can be but one infinite and all-inclusive God-Life, which infolds and encompasses all created expression, in earth and sky and sea. The life of the crystal, the flower, the bird, the beast, the child, and the life of you and me, is the same all-inclusive life which is God-Life. Therefore, instead of thinking of the bird's life, or the child's life, think of it only as the one God-Life—that Life which is, indeed, the All-in-all.

In my booklet *God Is All*, this idea of the one Life is taken up and explained specifically, and many are the letters testifying to the light and the help received therefrom. Life which is God, and which is the only Life there is, is complete and perfect, lacking absolutely nothing. It is undefilable as well as immortal; it is Substance and Reality, back of all existence and of all creation whatsoever.

So wherever you see life, see it as God's presence with us; see God about us everywhere. And think of life not as being multiple or separate, nor personal, but as the *one* Presence, the *one* All-in-all. Then shall you see, and can accept as a certainty, that life is full and glorious, is perfect, is complete, is immortal and everlasting, without change, impermanence or imperfection of any kind.

In the dream-belief we may see our happiness as in certain personalities, our wealth as in personal affairs, and our health as in a personal body; then, thus self-deceived, we appear as human beings. But when we accept the one God-Life, the one God-Body, and the one Self as the Christ, we see our wholeness, happiness and wealth in Him as *ours* now and forever. Then the unreal vanishes and is forgotten, days of darkness disappear, and Lo! peace and joy are found in our real Self at last.

Look unto Me, Turn unto Me, Come unto Me, is ever the call of the still, small Voice of the one

45

Christ-Consciousness to us each. Turn away from the dream that Life is divisible and that there are many human minds and bodies. Turn away from the belief of chance and change, of loss and limitation, of good and evil. Let your understanding of life coincide and coalesce with Mine; let your personal sense of separation be lost, or swallowed up, in the rarefied vision and conviction of My supreme and supernal Selfhood as the *only* Presence there is—which is Love, everlasting.

Since in us is the ability to "Choose ye this day whom ye will serve," then also in us is the ability to be conscious of our Christ-Reality—to see Life as Life is; to see Love as Love is; and to see and feel this Love-Life to be everywhere. In us is the ability to give up the dream of double-mindedness and see ourselves merge, as it were, with the Christ-Self which intuitively hears, "Son, all that I have is thine."

A surrender of false sense is accomplished in proportion to our loving desire to place God *first* in our lives, in our affections, and in our affairs.

The great truth of being is that Love-Wisdom is forever the I AM THAT I AM—the one whole Consciousness aware of Itself as perfection and completeness, lacking nothing. This Love-Wisdom Consciousness, besides which there is none else, knows that all is done, all is finished, all is good, all is here, nothing could be added to, nor taken from, the one radiant I AM.

Into this Love-Wisdom Consciousness no evil could enter, no distortion, no sense of lack, loss or interruption of any good. It is the circle of the one completely perfect Being of infinite ideas and their manifestation in time and space. Though our sense of life may be that there is evil, that there is lack, loss, limitation everywhere visible about us, this is due to an imperfect and erroneous sense which exists only because we have not seen ourselves as perfect in the Father's house, fully returned to the "One altogether lovely."

Let this truth that we are ever in the Father's house, never having left it, burn as a living beacon within you, and as the Self-revealing Light has already disclosed, It will bring you to that state of realization which is called "the Christ." Here light is ever-present, and you hear the welcoming words, "This is My beloved Son, in whom I am well pleased."

Jesus was the Christ because he never left the Christ state of knowing and being. This is why *Jesus* and *Christ* are one, and not two beings, as often supposed; for Jesus was never a prodigal, as portrayed in his parable. He always was, and still is, the Christ.

He gave himself to us and for us, that we might see him as he is, and seeing him as he is, we might be like him, the perfect One. "I am Alpha and Omega," said he, "Behold, I make all things new."

47

When you read the statement, "God or Christ is within you," what does this mean? Of course it cannot mean that God or the real Man is located anywhere in the body, for the *I* cannot be localized, since It is the Unconditioned. God is both within and without all things; and so to stress the statement that God is *within us*, and that only here shall we find Him, would give room for the assumption that the *I* is located in the body, which is not true.

Why look elsewhere for that which is so close to you, even closer than breathing? "You look for Me as located in things or bodies, in books and teachers, in thoughts and reasons," remonstrates the Christ, "and you think of Me as being within churches and doctrines. You will find Me when you seek for Me *with all your heart*—and your health, your wealth, your perfect unlimited good are all at that very place where you find Me, for I am your Self."

Also to place the *I* as *within* even the real Self would localize and limit It. Take for a helpful illustration another example of a sleeper and his dream. Suppose while he sleeps in New York, he dreams that he is on the streets of Boston. To say that the *I* is in New York, and not in Boston, would be to localize and limit the Unconditioned and Unlimited.

While this man walks, apparently, in Boston, the *I* is right at hand, and as close there as It ever could be in New York. Is this not so? To him who thinks he is in Boston, his identity is still not far off, but right wherever he finds himself. If someone in his dream asked him for his name, he would probably answer correctly. He would know his identity even in his dream.

Take another view of the sleeper. Suppose that while he sleeps, some friend carries him out of his room. Where, then, is that self which is his waking state? Did the friend take or leave it when he carried him from the room? Certain it is that no part of him remained behind. The self of the waking state cannot be separated or detached from him even in his sleep: for sleep or awake it is with him, and more—it is *he*, himself.

In any place, circumstance, condition or dream, wherever man is, *there* also is his real Self. The more we become intuitively and spiritually certain that, "I and my Father are one," the sooner shall we understand and utilize our power and glory, become one with His law of life and love, and learn how to function in the Self of the waking state.

Even though we may be deluded, or be entertaining a false belief, our identity is ever with us, for as the Scripture declares,

Whither shall I go from thy Spirit? O whither shall I flee from thy presence? If I ascend up into heaven, Thou art there: If I make

49

my bed in hell, behold, Thou art there. Yea, the
darkness hideth not from Thee.

It is an utter impossibility to become severed
or separated from the Self.

Life, Spirit, the *I* is not localized in the body,
even though life and body are one. You may say:
But the body dies, while life is eternal? Yet life
continues to manifest a body. How could it be
otherwise? What if the figure five be erased from
the blackboard—cannot another five, which is
really the same one, be put in its place? And
obviously, is not the second five identical with the
first one?

We shall always have a body, and it will be in
the form which reveals our individual sense and
feeling and point of awareness. The forms change
because they only clothe our state of belief, and
may even be erased from view; yet inevitably
another form, or another view of the real form,
will be present and occupied by us.

The form will continue to change "from glory
to glory" until we manifest the real body of Light,
which we express when we rise to the Christ state
of knowing: for when we reach the Christ state of
light, or knowing, simultaneously we shall manifest the Christ state of body, or the real body of
Light.

I AM THAT I AM is unlimited Spirit, encompassing, as It does, all forms. Back of the body is

the I-AM-SELF, and back of the I-AM-SELF is the infinite I AM THAT I AM. The I-AM-SELF is the real Self which will ever remain the same—"the Son, which is in the bosom of the Father."

How can we hope to express the form of ageless beauty, wholeness and harmony, if we are believing it impermanent and capable of all sorts of limitations—yea, even of death? This would place us in belief right back again as mortal human beings, would it not? We should see that the Christ encompasses the only body there is, and so, lovingly, with this perception, conform our thoughts thereto.

It is certain that we cannot separate Self and Body, calling one Spirit and the other matter, and see them in the Self-revealing Light. Ever thus speaks your I-AM-SELF: Turn to Me in full surrender of any personal self, any personal thoughts and feelings, as well as the unhappy dream that you have left Me. A dream is never reality, and seeing this fact you will know yourself to be where you have always been and shall ever continue to be—one with Me, the Self.

Many of you in deep earnestness and agony of soul, yearn for Me but do not find Me, because you search for Me as though I were afar off. Yet even feeling but a glow of light within and about you, know that you are then feeling Me, and learn to cultivate such feeling. Beautiful music, lovely scenery, inspirational lines of poetry, and sweet companionship with those who live the truth as you do, all these touch the heart, because they speak of the infinite Self-harmony, the real Being—the I-AM-SELF. They enlighten and inspire you, delivering to you the enjoyment of the eternal moment, the *now* of eternity.

So take time each day to rest and feel the peace and glory which is the manifestation of the Holy Ghost in you. Soon you will learn how to contact Me consciously, how to feel My presence at will, and so continue to live joyously in the kingdom.

In the language of the heart, which you can hear and understand, *I* come and speak to you. When you hear Me it is as though all of you as a personality were blotted out, and there were only Me.

Has any earthly joy brought you such radiant light and glory, such peace and wonder unspeakable, as such moments with Me? And *I* shall continue to be your comfort and joy, your Saviour and Deliverer forever and ever.

Every one today is searching for a way, a method, a definite road to travel where he will be able to experience continuous good and feel certain that he will never fail.

Yes, there is such a way! "I AM the way," of peace and power, of certainty and security. I AM the Self-revealing Light, purifying, uplifting, inspiring—bringing into view the perfect, original man and universe.

THE I-AM-SELF

Dear reader, are you hungry for the true bread of life? Then are you willing to give up the belief that you are separated in some way from the source of this heavenly manna—the real man who is, in very truth, *your Self*?

Why remain longer in the belief that you sojourn in a far country where the husks of lack, loss and limitation are your daily fare? You are not of that world at all, for "Ye are children of the Light."

Really, you are not on a physical plane; you are not in a fleshly body; you have no human form; you are not subject to man-made laws or beliefs.

Really, you are of the eternal substance. The mind you have is that mind which was also in Christ Jesus. Your only body is the body of light. Your very being is the radiant I-Am-Self.

But if you believe otherwise, and feel that you are living in and depending upon a material world of time and place, life and death, good and evil, then to you it appears so, and your ever-existent good, though never actually separated from you, is nevertheless hidden from your sense and sight;

for where your state of awareness is, there also will be your experience.

In that mental journey, which is the belief of being in a far country, back to the recognition that we have never been absent from the Father's house—many steps are to be taken. To think thoughts of health, wealth and success, even under a false impression that this may be done with a personal human mind, has been one of these steps, without a doubt. But now the night-mists are lifting and the new day dawns more clearly.

Any method of thinking, apart from the conscious knowledge of possessing *now* the Christ-Mind, to which "all things are possible," cannot deliver the full peace of God, nor the true, as well as lasting satisfaction to be found in the Master's statement, "I am the way; I am the truth; I am the life."

Transcending and overarching the general belief that while one's mind is human he must still think divinely with it, there comes a higher concept and deeper insight, which is that we should give no heed to a belief that our mind is "human," but on the contrary, we should take the position that our mind is divine, and thus, naturally, we think divinely with it. Such right vision and divine insight will surely bring us to the Horeb-height—that mountain of God where we behold and know Him as the I AM.

As we rise to the position that there is but *one* God, and hence but *one* Mind, we see there is not, and never could truly be, a so-called human mind or mentality; moreover, it is not by spiritually educating a fictitious human mind that we come into the divine, but quite the contrary is true— whoever shall lose his *belief* in a mind other than the one God-Mind shall find this *very* Mind to be his own.

It was a selfish belief, instead of a separate human mind, which prompted the son, in Jesus' parable, to desire to leave his father's house. And, later, the feeling of tender, yearning love in his heart brought back to him the awareness of his eternal unity, or oneness, with the Father, and hence, with the original perfect man which he was. And, dear reader, this same true awareness will likewise bring us back.

All thoughts of genuine value to man in this world have come to him through inspirational or intuitive knowing and feeling, which is the natural activity of the one perfect Mind within us all.

Spiritual illumination and inspiration come when we gladly surrender and shut out everything of self and of the world, in order that we may hear God's voice. The heavenly promise is then renewed and fulfilled—"I will instruct and teach thee in the way which thou shalt go."

The truth of Being does not come to man in order to destroy any evil anywhere, but it comes to him that having caught a glimpse of it he may hunger and thirst for his real Self, the radiant I AM. Hear, O my people everywhere! The hidden, inner man of the heart is none other than *your* Self! And, moreover, is your perfection right now. Indeed, this perception is the "well of water springing up into everlasting life."

The absolute teaching is not an abstract philosophy, nor some impossible and impractical transcendentalism, as often supposed, but delivers the accurate and intelligent understanding that one should give no heed to a self-imposed human mind, but instead, *identify himself with his real Self* in which is vested all-victorious power.

To you who are ready to leave a far country, I come. "No man cometh unto the Father but by me," his true Self, the Christ of God. This real Self, the perfect man, is *your* actual Being—you, as you *really* are—and is found as you turn in full surrender of *a self-imposed* mind and resultant thoughts to God.

You are not a mortal man at all; instead, you are ever one with Light, Love and Power. Hence what will it profit you, though you gain the homage of all men and fulfill all your human desires, if you still have unrest and yearn for peace? So perceiving that "I, of mine own self, can do nothing," the awakening process has begun.

Where *is* the real man about whom so much has been written and taught? Where does he live?

How is he related to you who are here, now? He is not located off in space somewhere, nor in some other place or world, for verily, he is to be found exactly at that place where you are this very instant. Thinking of the real man as afar off, or on another plane of consciousness, veils your vision to the supreme fact that he, the real man, is *you*, just where you are. For until man comes to himself, identified with his original perfect state as perpetually existing and intact now, how can he ever expect deliverance from a sleeping state called "mortality" and all that it includes?

Therefore "Cease ye from man, whose breath is in his nostrils, for wherein is he to be accounted of?" Isaiah had evidently discovered this essential step to take, and so should we all. Nor did Jesus concern himself with the right and the wrong thoughts of mortals, or men in dreams, but knowing himself to be the real man, and likewise they as well, he spoke from this understanding of reality, and all things were revealed to *be* as he commanded.

Can anyone but yourself let go of your own false believing? Can anyone but yourself rise out of your own self-deception? Jesus came to you and to me to show us a way out of such a dilemma of human existence. He penetrated its enigma by revealing the fact of our *preexistent* Christ-estate of mind and body. Thus he demonstrated that man need no longer be victimized by selfish beliefs, but may rise and come forth as from death to life, from being lost to being found again.

But to do this, he must come to himself—he must come to see who and what he *really* is.

Can there be darkness when light is present? Or can one sleep while he is awake? Obviously, then, it is no more possible for mental darkness or a dream of sin, sickness and limitation to continue to reign in our sense and thought when the light of our divinity breaks in upon us and abides. You are never actually in a dream, no matter how long you may be thinking you are. The man you think you are in a dream typifies the unreal mortal man, and the man awake typifies the preexistent real state— the original perfect man. Whether you are awake or asleep, whether you are aware or unaware of it, you are ever the same man, namely, God's spiritual, perfect man: *there is none other.*

The source of a problem is incorrectly placed, or not traced back far enough, when it is said to originate in false thinking, for where and in whom did such thinking begin?

Sin and ignorance, which are generally supposed to cause sickness and limitation, are after all, but dreams of the man who went to sleep, or who did not remain consciously aware of the truth of his being. And it is this very man who must now lay hold of his ever-existing real state and so prove the *nothingness* of such sleep. Can you see this stupendous fact, now, for yourself? There could be no sin without a sinner, no belief without a believer, no sleep without a sleeper, and no claim without a claimant. That was an utter impossibility. So until man surrenders an illusion, knowing it to be such, how can he possibly be liberated from it?

The way lies within yourself. You must become aware of your preexistent Self as the Self you manifested before going into a false state. Then the light of your divinity will surely waken you to behold the futility of ever attempting to make over a dream and yet leave man asleep!

This clearer and fuller understanding of man will make new demands upon us all. The requirement facing each of us today is that we relinquish absolutely the foolish notion that our health, peace or prosperity depends upon any personal thought-taking method, and instead, understand thoroughly that our good abides in us, *the true Christ-Self*, and nowhere else. And we are this man *consciously* to the degree that we put off the old beliefs and put on the new understanding.

We may temporarily dream and seem to lose awareness of ourself as the original spiritual man of God's creating, but every dream has an end. So our common dream of separation from our true Selfhood, in which we all participate, will come to a close for each of us as we see and acknowledge the one Mind, and no other, to be ours here and now; our life to be the one eternal and immortal verity; and the real man to be none other than our Self right where we are, *when so understood and expressed.* And so may this prove to each of us to be the glorious truth and radiant light which Jesus promised would set us free.

It is absolutely certain that God made everything out of His own perfection, and hence, all was, and still is, good and perfect. In this light we see that we are and must be spiritual and perfect— and more, we are Spirit and Perfection, for the Scripture reads, "That which is born of the Spirit is Spirit."

But to accept this fact intellectually or to truly see it inspirationally are two distinctly different viewpoints. To you who are ready to let go all personal methods in exchange for *the way,* Lo, to you *I* come, and *I* am with you always.

Now you can say, "I know that I AM! I know that my health, my harmony, my perfection, my happiness and my abundance of every good are not located in my body or in my affairs, but only in my real Self, myself *awake*—the I-Am-Self. Here abide my unalterable, undefilable health and wholeness; my perfect spiritual senses and their distinct activities; my ever conscious awareness of Reality as all there is; and my complete experience of every good thing.

Therefore, seeing this supernal fact, my desire should be, and is, to cease believing that my health is dependent in any way upon a physical form or even upon a spiritual form, or body. Though my form may still appear to be physical, I shall know that nevertheless I am ever one with the I AM THAT I AM; and hence, as Jesus said at one time, so may I say at this time, "Suffer it to be so now." The appearance of form as physical need in no way deter, interrupt or hinder my conscious awareness that: any form or body expresses but does not contain Me, the I AM, and therefore has no power to limit the wholeness which *I* am.

My sight and hearing, my tasting, smelling and feeling, are also in and of my radiant Self, the Christ-Man. They are perfect in eternity, from everlasting to everlasting. Nothing in and of a so-called physical plane, and its man-made laws and theories, can in any way interfere with, change, deform, distort or limit my spiritual senses, for they are no part of the body of the dream-world, but are wholly in the Christ-Self, the I AM, eternally one with God.

Now, dear reader, why do you need to longer feel the necessity of a method of taking thought whereby you may attempt to make changes and corrections (called healing) in your physical appearance? Is it not more intelligent to see and understand that your health is *never* in or of *any* body, but belongs only to the spiritual, perfect Man whom you already are?

The only necessary change or correction, therefore, should be made *in your sense and feeling, in your apprehension and understanding;* then your preexistent original estate of perfection will become true and real to you here and now. Could that which is true ever change? Or could Reality ever be less than It was always?

Why not transcend all ways and means of healing, changing, correcting or destroying thoughts or things and take the high vision of Reality—the vision of *being* the I-Am-Self, the vision of seeing this Self as a fact *now?* In proportion as you see and feel Reality to be operative here and now, and insofar as you can, live in harmony with It, you change, as it were, from the state of sleep to that of being awake and aware.

The Self-revealing Light shows us that we take conscious possession of the real, divine Mind when we see that it is truly the *only* mind, and so discard our thought of any other. Thus we go on thinking and feeling rightly, just accepting the simple fact that it is the mind of Christ which is doing it all.

In this way we learn more about how to multiply our good, since, with the divine Mind to which all things are possible, it is natural to have and enjoy the things which our heart desires. The *here* and the *now* is all that we are consciously aware of, for how could we live in the future, or in any place other than just where we are? This, then, is the time and the place where we multiply and replenish our good, for the I-Am-Self is here and never absent at any time.

When you make a declaration, affirmation or statement of what you wish to do, or what you desire to bring to pass, remember this paramount fact: spiritual things must be *spiritually* conceived and brought forth. Therefore, when you think, do not feel that it is a human mind you are using with which to bring about some special good, but as the man of God, the I-Am-Self, know that you are thinking with the Christ-Mind, and you will inevitably bring forth what is rightfully yours. Then your word, spoken as by the divine Mind, is your authority that it shall not return to you void, but shall go forth and multiply your good. This was Jesus' authority, and likewise may be yours.

You are consciously at-one with the divine Mind to the degree that you see, feel and express It, and believe in no other. Acting in the knowledge that this Mind is all-knowing and to It all things are revealed, state or declare your wish or need, and leave it with this Mind to fulfill, or bring to pass.

Back of us, around, above and within us is Power—infinite, invincible, and almighty. "I AM the real Man, at-one with the Father," is the cry of the soul singing its way into the full realization that "All power in heaven and in earth is given unto me." You are of that which is ever "above." Therefore your perception should be that Spirit includes your good and is ceaselessly blessing you. Spirit denotes the real substance; and the spiritual universe refers to creation as it really is: good, perfect, harmonious, incorruptible and eternal.

To repeat: The mind of Spirit should be considered the only mind, and you should relate yourself to It by your recognition of It as the real and the true, and hence the *very* mind which you are using now with which to think your good and true thoughts. You should also see and acknowledge that this mind is power, is light, is wisdom, and is love which never faileth.

Your vision determines your thinking. Your vision determines your feeling. Your vision determines your action. Your vision determines the multiplication of your good. Therefore, to experience the perfect creation, which all must do, you should begin with the perfect vision: I Am the Self. Not, I am John or Mary Jones, but *I Am the Self*, the Christ-Man. And you should say this as the living fact and not merely as a mechanical affirmation.

The I AM THAT I AM infinitely individualizes Itself as the Christ-Self, or I-Am-Self, each indivisible identity being capable of the full realization of his inherent wisdom and intelligence, hence his ability to multiply and replenish his sense of perfect creation. With clear vision and open heart, we now proceed to learn more about how such multiplication is to take place.

Working from the principle of the one Mind, the one Power, the one Spirit-Life, take the position as the I-Am-Self, instead of I am John or Mary Jones, and with this vision make your wish for that thing which you desire to have, and which your own Mind informs you is right and good for you to bring to pass. Remember, you are thinking with that Mind to which nothing is impossible, and with the Love which never faileth.

The I AM THAT I AM is the infinite powerhouse wherein the ever-existent good is generated and maintained. According to Genesis, God declared, "Let the earth bring forth grass ... Let the waters bring forth the moving creatures ... Let the earth bring forth the living creatures. And it was so." The command, you see, was *definitely* stated for the desired thing: Let there be this particular thing! "And it was so."

Many people are uncertain of their desires, and so change them from day to day, whereas we should form definite ideas and clearly state them, for such is the prerogative of the divine Mind. So always, when and wherever possible, determine and speak the definite idea. A wish, aim or desire, stated plainly, will bring forth "after his kind," for to every seed there is a corresponding body, or manifested form, which is creation.

One may ask: But how am I to know that what I wish is right and best for me to have in my present experience? The answer to this question is:

You cannot really know unless you are aware that you are associating yourself only with the divine Mind, and so from the standpoint of this Mind your desire must be right.

This is why, first of all, you should identify yourself with that state called the Christ, or the I-Am-Self, for he is ever one with God, and to him all good is possible.

Any desire of the true Self, or of the one Mind, is right and good and capable of being brought forth into visible manifestation as illustrated in the first chapter of Genesis, as well as in Jesus' life and miracles. As you identify yourself with the divine Mind, and no other, naturally you will begin to desire only those things which are right and best for you to have in your present experience. Your desire for some certain thing, therefore, will be proof to you that it is for you, since both the desire, as well as the experience, proceed from the same Mind. The I-Am-Self and the divine Mind are one and inseparable.

The questions may then be asked: How can the divine Mind, or Spirit, create material things? Is not the thing created, or which is brought to pass, verily material? To the one Mind, or Spirit, all creation is spiritual. Spirit could not create materiality, although limited vision calls it so.

Let us take, for instance, the lesson found in the New Testament where Jesus multiplied the loaves and fishes. Here the disciples brought to him the two loaves and few fishes as representing all the food available. This was *their* vision. But Jesus "looked up into heaven" and gave thanks. Jesus lifted his vision higher than human sense would allow.

To human sense—that is, to those who were not yet aware that they had never departed from their Father's house, and so were ever associated with infinite plenty—the supply of food was limited; and to this sense also it was material.

Jesus lifted his vision above human sense. The very food which they thought material and limited, he blessed. He placed a different interpretation upon it altogether, for the right discernment of Spirit ever beholds the inexhaustible and illimitable supply of thoughts and things. He saw in the loaves and fishes his own concept of food, and to him it represented spiritual good which may be increased or multiplied wherever one may be, according to the desirable amount needed, even were the necessity present to feed five thousand people.

To those who partook of the food, no doubt this spiritual expression looked exactly the same as their familiar so-called material loaves, whereas Jesus saw it as the manifestation of spiritual ideas. To the materialist, all things are material; to the spiritually-minded, all things are in and of Spirit.

For this reason, many find the increase of their good so difficult: they are attempting to multiply spiritually the very things which to them are material, instead of multiplying spiritual ideas, spiritually. It may seem to take time, and one may need to exercise patience with himself in order to learn how to translate *his sense of things* from a material basis to the spiritual and real.

"Ye must be born again," is still the explained process of regeneration as taught by the Master who knew all things. "Ye must be born of water and of Spirit." Not born again of materiality—of time, place and limitation. Remember, a far country is not a place nor a plane, but a state. We are therefore to leave one state—a state of falsely believing that we are material beings in a material world—and we are to take on the true state, the state of truly seeing that we are the real Man ever at-one with the real Mind. This is to be born again, born of water—purity and receptivity, and born of Spirit—Truth and Reality.

We are not to leave one material viewpoint for another material viewpoint which may seem an advanced one; but we are to leave the state of seeing things materially to seeing things spiritually. And in order to do this, we are to raise our eyes (vision) to heaven, reality. We are to get a new and true viewpoint.

Here on earth is where you should, and can, multiply your good. Here on earth, with spiritual awareness and right vision, is where you may bring to pass your heart's desire: for the spiritual ideas—wealth, abundance and prosperity—stand back of all your desires for supply, and so may be brought into visible form to the degree that you see them as they are, acknowledge and accept them.

You are therefore to leave the belief of being material, or mortal, for the true understanding of yourself as spiritual and immortal. Once establishing *yourself* in this right and true position or state, it will then also become easy and natural to establish your world and your affairs in their rightful places. To the spiritually minded, all is Spirit and Its spiritual accompaniment. Should your desire be for a strong, healthy, active body, such a desire is good and right; and if you are certain that it arises in you, the I-Am-Self, instead of John or Mary Jones, then your desire will be consummated. You should remember that the form and action of the real Self must be like unto It in all ways. The I-Am-Self and the I-Am-Body are one, for Life includes Its specific, perfect form. Thus as you identify yourself with the I AM, you likewise identify your form or body with perfect action, health and harmony.

Instead of thinking of the body as a dependent material object, think of it as simultaneously existing with the perfect Self, which you are, and consequently good. Instead of seeing the body as limited by man-made laws, understand it to be eternal, changeless, complete and perfect in action, feeling and form, because ever-existing with the one perfect Life and Love which you are, and which includes all.

Some consider themselves material beings with material bodies. Others, having raised their vision, believe that they are spiritual beings, but that they still express material bodies. In the Self-revealing Light it is seen that in our real state we are each not only the perfect spiritual Self, but also the perfect spiritual body.

From first to last the body should be seen and thought of as included in the perfect Self, and then it will easily be seen that all that ever needs changing or correcting is one's point of view. Thus as this is changed from belief to understanding, automatically one's world seems to change also; and whereas before there seemed to be discord, now harmony is expressed; and, whereas before there seemed to be lack and limitation, now plenty and abundance are expressed.

In this way reality, or the perfect creation, comes to light. You should therefore ever keep the vision of reality before you—reality here, there, everywhere; and never declare anything which you do not wish to see manifested. Reality includes you, the perfect I AM, or spiritual Self; you, the spiritual and perfect body; and you, the spiritual and perfect universe. For nothing exists *to you* outside of your Self.

At some point in every one's progress he will learn this real truth about himself, body, and universe, and will leave all else to lay hold upon this reality, which is his Father's house, and also his own.

Verily, the Self is the way to wholeness and harmony, to success and prosperity: for our Self is truly the light of the world. We should therefore sing praises to this glorious Self, our own I AM, ever one with God, the Father. "Put ye on the Lord Jesus Christ"—accept *as your own* the true (Christ) state—that perfect state of knowing, feeling and being which originally you had with the Father before the dream-world began. *In no other way can you personify the real or Christ-Man.*

Do not attempt to bring the perfect state of being into the mortal dream as though by so doing to repair the dream-conditions (while you are left to do further dreaming), but step out of the dream, as it were, by taking possession of your true Christ state into which no dream can possibly come. "They which are the children of the flesh (thinking as in a dream) are not the (real state of the) children of God."

You cannot return to the Father except by *first* returning to the perfect, real state, since this very state is the Christ, which is all-inclusive—eternally one with God. Paul writes very illuminatingly in the following verses:

"The head of every man is Christ; and the head of Christ is God ... Now ye are the body of Christ, and members in particular ... Christ is all, and in all."

Thus we cannot return to the Father except by returning to the Christ—the position of perfect being which is eternally one with God, even as the rays of light are one with the sun. The rays collectively represent the Christ, the Self-revealing Light, of which each one of us is a member in particular. Here we see why Peter declared so inspirationally to Jesus, "Thou art the Christ," because he saw that man operating in the Christ state is the Christ-Man.

"In Christ shall all be made alive." Verily, as we operate in this, our real state of knowing and expressing, we shall all be alive to our perfection as changeless and eternal, free from any mortal dream. "In him (the Christ state) dwelleth all the fullness of the Godhead bodily. Ye are (now, as in the beginning) complete in him," and so need only to take conscious possession of this eternal truth, and insofar as you can, live and act therein, to be set free from the mortal dream.

"Therefore, if any man be in (the) Christ (state) he is a new creature—(verily, the Christ-Man, the I-Am-Son); old things (of the dream) are passed away, behold, all things become new (as they were originally) ... No man cometh unto the Father but by Me"—the only way to the God-Consciousness

73

is through the Christ state, for "without me, (the true state of knowing, feeling and expressing) you can do nothing"—for only because you are not fully conscious of your real state, nor fully operating in it, does the dream of bondage and limitation persist.

This is the very truth which we should bring to that man who is called a mortal. When he comes to us for help we are to say to him, "You are not of this world. You are not of perishable flesh and blood. You are not both good and evil. You are not intended to experience death, but only life. You are God's perfect man exactly where you stand. You need only to feel this and live in harmony with it, and you will begin experiencing it."

Truly, until one comes to see himself as he is, he will never leave a far country of dreams and fables. When you come to yourself, you see who you are, and seeing this, you naturally see what body you have, what universe you live in, what power you make use of, what mind you utilize and what life you are living, feeling and experiencing. With such transformation of sense and view there also appears a corresponding transfiguration of body and affairs.

Does the Christ-Self exist because of what you, personally, think or feel? Does the real man, or man in his real state, know about Spirit and flesh, good and bad, or about time and place, sin, sickness and death? What is it that the I AM knows? It knows: I AM, and besides Me there is none else! It knows, "I am in the Father, and the Father in me." Thus I AM ever one with the I AM THAT I AM.

Say it over and over, sing it softly to yourself: I AM THAT I AM. Lovingly, earnestly, expectantly. Do not attempt to define what it means, nor analyze your feeling, but just say it, and it will begin to reveal itself to you, for the I AM THAT I AM reveals Itself to me, to you, to all who say: I will arise and go unto my Self in my true state of being—where nothing can oppose me—nothing!

The I AM does not depend upon thought or feelings, times or places, conditions called sin and goodness, life and death, for Its existence: the I AM THAT I AM says: *I* am all power, *I* am all perfection. Do not confine Me to this or that idea or thought, word or saying. Do not limit Me to churches or ministers, to man or woman, to books or sentences. I AM THAT I AM, the Unconditioned, the Eternal One.

There is but the one I AM THAT I AM. There is not one big *I* and millions of smaller I's. One Life is all there is, even as one air is all the air there is. This one I AM THAT I AM includes granite heights, crystals, trees, flowers, birds, animals, man and all created things. Surrender, therefore, the *ifs, buts, whys* and *wherefores* for this absolute state of yourself—your radiant I AM, ever the Self-revealing Light.

The I AM does not concern Itself with your sins or limitations, with your past or future; does not concern Itself with your body or affairs, with your father or mother, your husband or wife, with your station in life, your color, age, nor education. The I AM concerns Itself only with *you*. Ever It declares: there is no cause or effect besides Me. I see no ignorance or darkness, no evil anywhere, for to Me there is nothing but Myself. I am the All-in-all.

I am found when all else fails; when all other means are of no avail, and when no thinking can find the way out. Lo, your extremity is My opportunity to prove to you *Myself* to be your All-in-all. *I* am present always, the never failing, Self-existent One. If you make your bed in hell, lo, *I* am there. If you take the wings of the morning and dwell in the uttermost parts of the sea, ever there *I* am, for *I* am with you wherever you are. *I* am *your* Self.

I am the Self which, apparently, you have wandered away from—but only as in a dream which you can readily see, if you will, has no substance at all. No dream can ever separate us, for *I* am with you wherever you are. *I* am with you in your sorrow, in your failure, in your defeat. *I* am with you in your joy, in your pleasure, in your success. What is darkness to you, shineth as the light to Me.

I am the Self to whom you now lovingly turn. None of your delusions affect Me. Ever *I* am at your side waiting only your awareness of Me, your recognition and realization of Me as your All-in-all, to set you free from any false belief in separation. When you leave all for Me, then shall you find Me. When you cry out yearningly from your heart to Me, then shall you hear My voice answering you: *I* am your hope of glory. *I* am your bright and morning star. *I* am the Lord, your God. *I* am *you*, your Self.

Acknowledge Me in all your ways. Acknowledge your Self in Its true position, and thus enjoy Its supreme ability and power in all your undertakings. See your radiant Self as verily the real man, about whom so much has been written for lo, these many years. See this Self, *your Self*, as the Christ-Self—all-victorious, pure, complete, supreme, triumphant in all things and in all ways.

As you have loved and praised, believed in and worshipped Jesus, the Christ, as the perfect and adorable One, even so must you now think of and consider *your* Self—for, dear reader, the Self of Jesus and the Self of you and of me is not separate or different, but is, in very truth, the same: "That they all may be one; as Thou, Father, art in me, and I in Thee, that they also may be one in us."

"If a man walk in the night (unillumination) he stumbleth, because there is no light in him" (John 11:10). Our righteousness shall be brought forth as the light if only we will be receptive to progressive ideas, to new revelations, and to the ever-revealing light of the Self. Many who read these lines know that they are not advancing as they should, nor as they once did, yet they feel that they are striving harder than ever before; that they read and study the books of truth faithfully; that they are sincere in their declarations and prayers; still they do not progress in demonstration nor understand why this is so.

Arise and come forth! ever calls the Self. As new leaves in spring push off the old ones from the tree, so the new and more advanced ideas of truth which we apprehend and accept push away outgrown beliefs and theories. Most frequently, at first, we obtain the light through teachers and books, but this same spiritual illumination may also come to us directly from God, the I AM THAT I AM, without the channel of any outer communication whatsoever.

It often happens that after many years of study one may seem to come to a standstill, to a place where he makes no further progress. It is apparent then that he needs fuller light, though perhaps unwilling to make this acknowledgment, even to himself. Then, again, fuller light may have been presented to him which he refused to listen to or accept.

Of course this refusal to progress must retard one's return to the Self, bind him to old positions outgrown, and close the door to the divine Truth which should always be kept wide open. As the sun shines on us all alike, so also revelation of the truth of our being may come to us all—to anyone who will receive it. Working with prescribed thoughts, as such, day after day, struggling with the repetition of sentences, no matter however true, keeps one in a far country where "no man gave unto him." Meanwhile, the realization is dawning that it is for all to come of themselves to the perfect radiant Self.

One must arise, welcome and follow the beckoning light, and so come to the perfect state where the Self really lives. In this way he finds the All-good, and all problems vanish.

Many are now in the process of such awakening. Our waking, or coming into the real state, is not instantaneous as in our waking from a night's sleep; for indeed, it seems to require much time with all of us; yet how grateful we should be that we are beholding the way, and ever we are gaining a better understanding of Jesus' life and teaching; that we have received so much help from others who have blazed the trail before us, and that this Self-revealing Light ever continues to shine upon us—to reveal and make Itself more fully known to us.

In these latter days it is to be expected that more abundant light will come swiftly and will break suddenly, perhaps, in full radiance upon the quickened senses, so that a complete awakening will take place. But until this event comes, we should do all we possibly can in the way of preparation for the way, the light, the resurrection, by acknowledging our real Self to be present with us right here on this so-called physical plane, for such, after all, is the true awareness.

Right here where we are expressing a so-called physical body, and right here where we have believed that we were using a so-called human mind, is the time and place where we are to see and claim the perfect Christ-Self, and no other, as the one Self of each and all of us. This is the truth which will surely set us free from any opposite beliefs. This one Self is the Self of us all, is the Son of God, the real man, and is "the one altogether lovely." Individuality is infinite in expression as you and I and every other man, woman and child. We each have a distinct individuality which expresses and makes manifest the one Christ-Self.

We read in the Bible that "in the beginning" God created man in His own image. He did not have diversified ideas about man, but completely perfect ideas of all that man is and includes. Each of us, then, whom God created, must be the personification of the perfect and original Man which is the Christ-Man. Jesus exemplified this creation perfectly.

As there is but one idea of mathematics, or as mathematics is one and not two, so Christ is one, and this one is called the perfect Self, or the real Man. And as we may each have and use all there is of mathematics and still all is left for everyone else, likewise one may express, use and manifest the one Christ-Man, and still everyone else may do the same.

When this illustration is clearly seen and understood, then you will apprehend and realize the oneness of the Christ-Man, and also his infinity. You will always have your distinct individuality; you will never merge, as it were, into another individual, but will ever express and experience the original spiritual man.

When we are commanded to, "Put ye on the Lord Jesus Christ," this means that we are to put on the Christ state, for this is the state which is Lord of all. As we put on the Christ state or function in this true state of knowing, feeling and expressing, we are the Christ-Man, and no other. We can put on "the new man" only by operating in our real and true position, for then, automatically, we become the real man of God's creating. "For it pleased the Father that in him (the real Christ-Man) should all fullness dwell." Jesus perfectly expressed man in God's likeness, for we read in John's gospel:

"And the Word was made flesh, and dwelt among us, and we beheld his glory, the glory as of the only begotten of the Father, full of grace and truth."

Thus Jesus was, and still is, the Christ. There are not many "Christs" any more than there are many mathematics. The word "Christ" means, primarily, *the perfect state* of spiritual being. *The Christ* is the state of knowing and being Perfection. When man expresses this Christ state, then he is called the Christ-Man. This Christ, or perfect state of being, exists potentially in every one of us. It exists the same as one's waking state exists in him even while he sleeps; nor could he ever be separated from it.

In the preceding chapter, "The Self-Revealing Light," it is clearly shown and explained how man's waking state exists in him even when asleep; how as he loses sleep by waking, he then *consciously* operates in that state. Thus as we lose a dream state by putting on the Christ state, or consciously operating in it, we experience reality.

Today, like the pendulum of a clock, we find ourselves swinging, as it were, between the position of the wakeful immortal and the self-imposed position of the sleeping mortal; and as St. Paul says, "It is high time that we awake out of (such) sleep." Indeed, the time is definitely here when we must see just what this sleep means and includes, for it was this very sleep which originally dimmed our vision of perfect God and perfect man and brought about all that we are unhappily experiencing today.

When man functions in his natural state, as God created him to do, he is then an immortal consciously aware of his true state of being in the kingdom of heaven. Should he choose not to remain in this state, however, as clearly illustrated by the rich man's son, he enters what the Bible calls a *mental sleep* where he is not fully aware of himself as he really is. Thus we see that though the son *may choose which state he will serve*, still the true state is always present and ever one with the Father, and the other state but denotes a mental lapse from the true and real, so constitutes the unreal state where unhappy and discordant conditions spring up.

When light is withdrawn from a room, the result is called darkness, and in precisely the same way, when we withdraw ourselves from the true state of being by becoming mentally asleep to the truth that we are ever the perfect man of God's creating, and so ever completely harmonious and lacking nothing, the result is then called mortality. Thus it is imperative that we waken and remain awake, to enjoy the peace and happiness of that true state where, actually, we are the light of the world.

How shall we place ourselves in this true state, as it were, so as to be the real man, here and now? Just our fervent and earnest desire to do this, more than to do anything else in the world, will immediately and effectively help to bring this about. When the heart really and truly desires, above all else, to live the true life of peace, loving-kindness and goodness, and so is willing to give up, so far as it is able, any contrary seeing, thinking and feeling, one instantly finds himself in that true state of being, even as upon opening his eyes from slumber, he immediately enters his daytime experience.

So, first of all, *lovingly desire* to live more fully in your true Christ state—that original and ever-existing state of perfect man, and long with all your heart to leave a selfish, self-indulgent state of seeing, thinking and believing in which we have all so long lingered. Let us come to the Father, now, and humbly say, "Father, forgive me, for I knew not what I was doing." Truly, such yearning, heart's desire to please God, as well as an utter willingness to abandon a false state of mental sleep, permits the light to stream in.

Present in and back of every created thing, is the real Life, the real Mind, and the real Being, of which things are only the symbols. Perfection is the original essence and spiritual nature of all that is. Back of a world of change, of impermanence, rests the Eternal which is the Unchangeable. Ever underlying the finite is the Infinite. Underlying our dream is the waking state of Spiritual consciousness. Underlying all falsity is the truth. Underlying death is life eternal.

What we call reality is God, existing without beginning or end, underlying all forms and all things, and the primal cause of them. Reality exists of and by Itself; It depends upon nothing, for It is the I AM THAT I AM. It abides invariable and constant in all things; It precedes and survives all changing forms, states and conditions.

This Reality for which everyone searches day after day (although he may know it not) is in and of nothing man invented. This is why so often he misses the way, because he is looking where Reality can never be found. He feels "a mighty famine," and foolishly continues looking for the substance of the All-good amidst the husks of materiality, hereby entangling himself more and more in the dream of a material existence.

"Look unto me, and be ye saved, all the ends of the earth; for I am God, and there is none else" (Is. 45:22). Such is that innermost call of Love, which each of us must, sooner or later, heed and obey.

Dear reader, begin now to answer to this greatest of all the demands made upon us, which is *to love*. Inspirational and intuitive thinking and feeling are not physical emotions nor the properties of a make-shift mentality, but they denote the conscious possession of that mind which was in Christ Jesus. Be assured of this from the revelation vouchsafed to you from on high.

Verily, we must find God to be Love—*in the heart of man.* The Bible uses this word "heart" as symbolical of the innermost and vital part of man, even as Jesus said, "Blessed are the pure in heart, for they shall see God." So counteract, or offset, the hold which past or present mistakes may have had upon you, by letting Love permeate your whole being; and It will generate, automatically, that right feeling which is called *forgiveness,* for this, Jesus taught, must precede light and illumination.

Love and forgive your enemies by looking through their mistakes to catch a glimpse of the radiant Self standing in their midst untouched by any mortal dream-appearance. From this place, which is holy ground, blotting out of memory that mortal-appearing man or woman who has treated you wrongly or unkindly, perceive that it is not this sinning appearance which you are bidden by Spirit to love. No, indeed! It is the Christ-Man whom you should recognize and into whose shining face you should smile, and whose hand you should clasp in understanding love.

Do this, beloved, that you may be the obedient Son of the Father; and upon you will dawn that light which is brighter than the sun; and if your limbs are fettered you will presently find them supple and usable again, and if restrictions have been placed upon your affairs they will be released, and you will walk in freedom; for where your loving feeling is, there shall your complete and happy experience be also.

The higher illumination and understanding reveals the fact that we are really not living on a material plane which would involve the necessity of destroying, either physically or mentally, our ever-increasing and multiplying problems, sorrows and limitations. What is termed a "plane" is really a certain state of awareness, instead of a place. This is what makes our freedom possible, because we need not move from one place to another, but merely from one point of awareness to another higher and more enlightening one, in order to become a new creature and exclaim, "Behold, all things are made new."

Thoughts which spring from Love inspire and elevate our aims and efforts, and draw us into the realization of our true estate. We may have believed that Truth or Mind is one entity, and Love is another, but the Self-revealing Light shows us that Wisdom and Love are but two aspects of the same Self. Love is perfected in Wisdom, and Wisdom is revealed in Love. So to seek for Wisdom or Truth as though It were separate from Love is to be unaware of one of the basic facts of Being.

Be still, O, so still. Endeavor to feel warm, pulsating love for God, for Self, for all. Let tenderness, forgiveness, unselfish goodness flood and fill you completely with their divine effulgence. Then light and peace will envelop you, and you will sing songs of joy and gladness. Inspirational thoughts, too, will come to you effortlessly, and Love will lift you above the sense of sleep and of twilight into that realm where it is always day, and where it is a joy just to live and to be.

Thus shall you understand that glorious saying, "He that dwelleth in love dwelleth in God and God in him." For you know that it is so.

We know that while standing in the light we could not be in darkness; just so, we know that knowing and feeling our place in the true Light, we cannot believe in or be conscious of the untruth, or unreality. And even though we may still appear to be in human form, now we know where we came from and who we are. Even while we live, apparently, in a so-called physical world, we may claim, and make good our claim, that we are the I-Am-Self living in the kingdom of heaven.

This is the spiritual vision which we must always utilize in order to see things correctly. When we rightly claim the actions, functions and organs of our body to be perfect now, which is the vision in the Self-revealing Light, we do not focus attention on a physical appearance, as though attempting to spiritualize what is called matter;

nor try to change any form from sickness to health or from disease to harmony, nor do we hold any false picture-form of body in thought while the true vision is ours.

Right where I am apparently expressing a discordant or limited condition of any kind, right here is where I am to realize and declare the very truth of myself as not material but spiritual, not matter but Spirit, since God, Spirit, is All-in-all. I am not dreaming now, but I am awake in the Light, and so I am partaking of Reality and Perfection. Truly and joyously, I love the fact of my continuous and uninterrupted harmony which is eternally mine, since I ever exist in the Christ who is one with God. I know that my remedy for any and all falsehood is the truth that discord of any nature is unreal since not of God, and that God and His perfection is present with and in me always. Inasmuch as troubles of all kinds are wholly mental and never, as it seems, physical, then by seeing, knowing and feeling Love, Perfection, Harmony to be God, who is All-in-all, and knowing that the Christ of God is right within me, having power, o'er all victorious, I know the mental dream will leave, since no darkness can abide in the light.

I am convinced that it is spiritually required of me that insofar as I am able, I must steadfastly and continuously endeavor to live my daily life and contact with people and things consistent with my spiritual idea and real feelings, for such consistent activity is the means to bring about my awakening. I now clearly understand and accept as true the words written in 1875 by a great spiritual teacher: "The body of Spirit is spiritual and not material. We shall be found Love, Life and Truth because we understand them." Thus, more and more, I am depending upon the Reality which I AM for my health, wealth and happiness, and less and less upon man and his mistaken laws in a far country.

I know that "Christ is the end of the law" of discord and all dreams of separation from Perfection. Thus as I function in this Christ, (which state is always within me) that is, as I remain worshipping, loving and living in the Christ state of light and understanding, I find that I am in the kingdom, I am at peace, I am filled with the glory of Harmony and Reality—verily, I am "hid with Christ in God" where no evil shall come nigh me. "And the Spirit and the bride say, Come. And let him that heareth say, Come. And him that is athirst come. And whosoever will, let him take of the water of life freely."

In the absolute teaching we deal with the Truth which is Reality without beginning or end. We deal with the true Mind, the true thoughts, the true body, the true universe, and the true Christ-Self, always.

Instead of trying to educate a mind to become divine and immortal, which, paradoxically, we had considered human and mortal, we can see now the folly of such a notion. From a higher point of vision all things appear different. Attempting to renovate or remodel our thinking so as to change a human mind into the mind of Christ is not the teaching of the I-Am-Light. Furthermore, holding in belief that the body is physical by nature, and still attempting to renew and remedy it by means of spiritual thinking, is not a true application of the absolute.

The only Mind that we should deal with is the one Mind back of every true and perfect idea. And the only body we should consider is the body which expresses naturally these ideas of wholeness. Then, automatically, we give up the notion of healing a human mind, or bringing the harmony of the I AM into a human body. We see the futility of it. We see as never before the great necessity to know and feel that there is but the one Mind, the one Body, and the one Life-expression; and that there is none else.

When apprehending reality, one will also learn to understand the nature of unreality. He will see with the vision of Spirit; he will know with the intelligence of Mind; he will feel with the heart of Love; and he will be satisfied that he is waking in His likeness.

This may be one of the reasons why many complain of failure or inability to demonstrate the truth in body and affairs—they are attempting to apply the truth of Being directly to sick bodies and sick affairs: whereas the truth can be applied *only* to vision, thought, sense and feeling.

Attempting to heal physical bodies or spiritualize human mentalities metaphysically, or by right thinking, overlooks the paramount fact that all discord, limitation and imperfection are totally *unreal*, because untrue! The eternal, real and true conditions *already exist* in the one Christ state, to be seen, accepted and utilized wherever vision is clarified sufficiently to thus behold the omnipresent Christ-Man.

"Behold, I come quickly, and my reward is with Me." As we rise to welcome the Self-revealing Light and behold the I-Am-Self, the entangling dream-shadows effortlessly slip from us. With winged feet we speed toward our goal—that Horeb height where the I AM THAT I AM stands revealed, and rapturously we exclaim with the apostle, "Beloved, now are we the Sons of God,"—now are we the Son-Self, the radiant I AM.

Realities Supernal

Each day those of us who are progressing onward and upward in the conscious awareness of realities supernal are becoming familiar with fresher ideas of the wonders of Life, and so are enjoying a correspondingly new and altogether satisfying experience: for former dreams are passing away. Said John the Revelator:

And I saw a new heaven and a new earth: for the first heaven and the first earth were passed away; and there was no more sea.

Divine Intelligence is ever progressing, and so continually reveals and unfolds to us the wondrous and illimitable ideas which constitute Its very Self-existence and Its state of perpetual activity throughout time and space. Love-Intelligence and Its mode of thinking is the only true Consciousness there is; and this is ours as we identify ourselves with the Christ-Self.

When we contemplate and associate ourselves with this eternal fact, we find ourselves losing our old personal habits of thinking and believing; they pass away, and behold, instead, we find ourselves refreshingly alive to the new and ever-inspiring ideas which make living so wondrously worth-while.

Unless life is becoming clearer and richer to us day by day, we are not progressing as we should, for we require the constant revelation of Truth to satisfy an ever-recurring need, just as pure, fresh water is essential in our everyday living.

Any book of an inspirational nature will be self-revealing if the reader brings to it a receptive heart. He will then receive bountifully of its rich message, its language will be easily understood and its ideas quickly assimilated. Heart speaks to heart naturally. The heart-books cannot be comprehended by those who are still in agreement with books appealing only to reason and intellect, any more than such books are of importance to the reader who hears and feels only through the heart.

The way of the heart is for those who have found the way to embody Love; for Love can easily make Itself understood to him who has found through experience that spiritual things must be *spiritually* understood. It is easy for the lover of Truth to accept the deep things of God, for indeed, the very truths which he reads seem to be springing right from out his own Being.

How true it is that practically all messages written from the heart are alike—all of them stressing, as they do, the necessity of the surrendered life, all of them calling attention to the *living* and *feeling* of the Truth rather than the mere formal thinking about It; well knowing that we will naturally think true and lovely thoughts if the heart and soul are right with God; whereas no amount of mere mental cultivation will ever touch the heart to make it burn within and so open it to the glad recognition of the indwelling Christ.

Here in this kingdom of eternal wonder and glory, *he*, the Christ-Self, is the *I* that I am. He is the eternal, unchangeable One encompassing me and all my affairs. By surrendering all, and returning to the Self-revealing I AM, I now know my being to be God-Being, my mind to be God-Mind, and myself the Christ-Self, forever.

Surrendering, day by day, any desire to worship or serve other gods while here in my Father's house of reality, I see and accept, love and adore all things as they are about me. I see that everything is as perfect as its Maker and Creator is perfect. I see Love encompassing and animating all living things, for I know that the one Love-Consciousness, and Its ever-revealing ideas, is the All and the Only.

This one Consciousness knows peace, joy, completeness and perfection forever and ever, harmoniously guiding and directing all things and governing the heavens and earth. Verily, Its immortal ideas from the least to the greatest originate and abide in the forever All-in-all; unalterable, ever-harmonious and complete.

Finally, here before our very eyes, all things will appear in their true form, and all inclination to wander, as in a sleep or dream, will leave us; for truly, as Paul said, "That which decayeth and waxeth old is ready to vanish away." Moreover, it is written that,

> God shall wipe away all tears from their eyes; and there shall be no more death, neither sorrow nor crying, neither shall there be any more pain: for the former things are passed away.

Our willingness to place ourselves on the right path and take the first steps forward marks our hour of departure from a far country of sleep to the true state of wakefulness, or awareness. Nor can any sin or sickness have power over us when we walk firmly on this highway—the way of holiness.

Instead of the mental state of chaos so apparent in the world today, there will be certainty and comfort. Instead of the longings and heartaches which vex us now, there will be indescribable harmony and peace. The fierce animals will no longer seem to be ferocious, for we are told that even the carnivorous wolf of today will then be found to lie down with the lamb.

The wolf also shall dwell with the lamb, and the leopard shall lie down with the kid; and the calf and the young lion and the fatling together; and a little child shall lead them (Isaiah 12:6).

The children of His love (and we are all as children in the kingdom) shall delight in them and find their companionship a constant source of cooperation and helpfulness; for here, in the Love-Kingdom, we give and receive of the infinite and illimitable bounties of love and understanding. Music, too, is heard all about us, for Life Itself is music, and rapturously we listen, to find ourselves in full rapport with Its perfect melody and rhythm.

Activity? Yes, indeed. We go joyously about our Father's business, which perpetually enables us to participate in His spiritual riches and the beauty of holiness; and the nearer we approach our native home, as our Christ-Self, the clearer becomes our vision and the more eloquent our praise.

We are truly aware that the senses of Spirit are in and of Spirit, not vested in any person or form. They are therefore imperishable, impeccable, and changeless, no longer controlled or influenced by man-made laws of the dream. The I-Am-Self includes the senses, the thinking, feeling and form—"that the Father may be glorified in the Son."

97

Indeed, to have believed otherwise was the original sin: for any belief of personal control, personal power or personal possession always leads away from that highway which is the way of wholeness. When beholding the oneness and the allness of Life and Its formations, of Consciousness and Its ideas, of Spirit and Its identification, we rise to new heights and then see realities supernal.

Here in this light we now see a so-called "mortal man" to be but a dream-presentation of the spiritual man, for it was *after* the son of God (the rich man's son) left his awareness of the I-Am-Self as ever one with the Father, and so as Self-sufficient always, that a so-called mortal appeared in his stead. The story reads that it was the son who was living right in his father's house who craved independence, and who consequently left the house of plenty, only later to contritely and rejoicingly return to it.

It should be seen that it was not a different man who returned, but the self-same man in a redeemed state of awareness.

The redeemed of the Lord shall return, and come with singing unto Zion; and everlasting joy shall be upon their head: they shall obtain gladness and joy, and sorrow and mourning shall flee away (Is. 51:11).

So shall it be with everyone, for our identity with the spiritual man can never change despite our long spell of sleep. Waking now to the Light, and to the realities It discloses, and claiming our identity as ever one with the Father, irrespective of dreams and falsities, we wait for Him to reinstate us in His and our home of eternal Joy and gladness.

Dear reader, are you now fully aware that God's man is really the *only* man there is? When the practitioner says to a mortal-appearing man, "You are spiritual; You are of God, You are perfect," he speaks correctly and states a fact, for dreams are never realities but unrealities only. Verily one's own identity and reality (though invisible to human sense) is always intact and present, even here where a mortal-appearing man is seen.

Surely, Jesus would not have given his life to save mortals! When Paul said that this mortal must put on immortality, although he referred to us all, he knew that only because of a sense of having lost our perfection do we *appear* mortal, but that we are always, in very truth, *immortals*. Hence, it is immortal man who is to waken from his dream that he is mortal; then what is termed mortality will vanish.

When it becomes generally accepted in the truth that a mortal-appearing man is an *effect*, and not, as has previously been considered, the cause of all mistaken beliefs and happenings, a great change will result in present-day teachings. Right along this line, a great teacher of the principles of true Being, wrote in her current textbook as follows: "When we wake to the truth of being, all disease, pain, weakness, weariness, sorrow, sin, death, will be unknown, and the mortal dream forever cease."

Note the words, "When *we* wake." Of course *we are the ones to waken for we are the ones asleep!* This same writer speaks of us frequently as "mortals" yet, not-withstanding, claims that we are "spiritual and perfect." This seeming paradox may now be explained.

As fuller revelation dawns, we see that it is God's man (for there is no other) rather than "mortal man" who entertains the dream of separation and so must waken and become disillusioned, (just as the prodigal did) and return to the truth of Being. When *we* lose the dream, naturally the dream itself, called sin, sickness and limitation of all kinds completely vanishes.

And the heavens departed as a scroll when it is rolled together and every mountain and island were moved out of their places (Rev. 6:14).

When this new viewpoint becomes apparent, man will understand clearly that he is here just as the prodigal son was in a far country; he came from his Father's house (believing he left it) and now (in belief) he returns to it.

One should see this new light so clearly that he will ever hold to it in thought and word, and now and hereafter understand mortality to be an unreal experience which must vanish *as man turns from that state.* How simple to now see clearly this hitherto perplexing paradox; how profound and far-reaching its application then will be!

Yet always he is the self-same Son who never left his Father's house. Jesus spoke so eloquently of that "joy that shall be in heaven over one sinner that repenteth, more than over ninety and nine just persons who need no repentance." If this sinner is not you and I, then who is he?

If anyone challenges the truth of this implied statement and believes that he has no connection with sin and its results, then why is he attempting to advance himself spiritually? Why is he seeking a more perfect sense of health, harmony or the abundance of good? *And why is he falsely appearing here as a limited human being?*

Who are you? "Now are we the sons of God." Yet, notwithstanding this fact, note again the words of the inspired John:

If we say that we have no sin, we deceive ourselves, and the truth is not in us. If we say

*that we have not sinned, we make him (Jesus) a
liar, and his word is not in us.*

Has not every one of us erred and so made
mistakes—yea, even grievous ones? To be sure we
have. Still the blessed truth is that we are the same
"sons" in the unreal sinful "here" as in the real
sinless "there," exactly as portrayed by the
prodigal in the parable. When one seeks and
searches for another world, another body, another
mind, another experience, as all do, experiencing
unrest and dissatisfaction, either he is refusing to
see and accept the original cause for such a
situation, and by so doing becomes unable to
subsequently free himself from it; or else he makes
a reality out of that which ultimately must be seen
as basically an unreality, since not originating in
God but only self-imposed.

The Jesus-Christ-Way is to frankly acknowledge any mistakes we may have made, repent of
them, and henceforth live and walk in the true
way. For as John said, "If we confess our sins, He
is faithful and just to forgive us our sins, and to
cleanse us from all unrighteousness."

To claim that we never fell from our original
position of perfection (instead of admitting that *in
belief,* this is exactly what took place) is self-
contradictory—which one's everyday efforts in
working in the truth disprove; moreover, this
results in delaying and prolonging one's liberation

from the mental dream state. Or, to make the claim, as the great majority do, that we did wander from perfection, yet not to see that such was not actual or real, but false mental belief only, and so temporal and unreal because of the impossibility of any separation to have ever taken place between Father and Son, keeps one in bondage to a lie.

Here, in this false state of sleep, you are struggling to waken, as we often do in dreams. You are studying spiritual books and teachings in order to do this very thing, are you not? And you desire (or should) above all else, to walk always in that path which Jesus revealed to be the road heavenward—the I-Am-Way, the I-Am-Light and the I-Am-Resurrection.

Paul said that we are "without excuse." He wrote to the Romans: "Because that when they knew God, they glorified him not as God, neither were thankful: but became vain in their imaginations, and their foolish heart was darkened." Hence, we see that we must now give up all vanity of a separated self—as though there *could* be any satisfaction for us outside the wondrous love of God, who gave us *all* He is!

No wonder we hunger and thirst to come back to the I-Am-Self and again worship Him, the I AM THAT I AM, as the fullness of our joy, the super-abundance of our good, and the completeness of our peace.

Paul, in his enlightening letter, continues: "Professing themselves to be wise, they become fools ... and worshipped and served the creature more than the creator." Foolishly we thought of our wonderful Self as *personal*, and of our luminous body as a separate entity. Instead of acknowledging the *oneness* and everlasting glory of the Father "in whom is no variableness, neither shadow of turning"—we put other gods before Him!

No wonder Jesus admonished all to *repent ... return ... reverse yourselves!* What else could ever redeem us?

And no wonder he reiterated again and again that the kingdom of heaven is within us, that is, we all have it in our own power to enter again that reality from which we have, seemingly, wandered so far away. Nor need we move hand or foot to do so. We need only turn to God in the full surrender of our foolish hearts, crying out from the depths of our contrition, "Father, forgive me and receive me, for I shall be satisfied only when I awake in Thy likeness; I will be at peace only when I am reinstated in Thy glory, for I fully realize that the Son of God, consciously expressing his inheritance in his Father's house, is my only real and actual state of Being."

Reverse yourselves, persisted Jesus, the Master-Teacher from on high. Reverse your desire from your willingness to remain estranged from your true Christ state to that of longing to return to it more than anything else in all the world. Begin today, now, to cultivate the desire for a full surrender of all your personal aims and ambitions, and feel the redeeming hunger and thirst for the everlasting love of God which is ever round and within you.

Then give all the glory to the great I AM THAT I AM, and withhold none of it for the personal self. Let your acknowledgment be: The Father in me, He is my All-in-all. Whatsoever I am, I am only because He is *all* of me, for "The Father is in me, and I in Him."

With what joyous, sensitive awareness I now feel the ring upon my finger — the symbol of my oneness with and inseparableness from the Father's house and the realities supernal. I see about me everywhere the familiar signs of abundance and profusion, and hear the joyous sounds of feasting and song. Exultingly I realize that I am waking to my Christ estate.

And what has brought me hither? My fervent desire to make the full surrender of self, my eager willingness to give all glory to God and acknowledge Him as my All-in-all, and my aim to seek nothing for myself outside of Him. Then, acknowledging myself as Spirit, Life, Truth and Love, I do so with the conscious awareness that my glory is the glory I had with Him before the world (of dream) was.

I am Spirit because He is Spirit, and He is all of me. I am perfect, complete and lacking nothing, because in Him I live, move and have my being. I am immune from all evil, from all lack and limitation, to the degree that I am aware that "He maketh me to lie down in green pastures; he leadeth me beside the still waters." Indeed, he is my Wisdom and my Love forever and ever.

To many it will be seen as a definitely new idea that Mind and Love are not two separate God-qualities but are united in one. Should one believe that he is responding to Truth, but only in a mental or intellectual way, he may then be certain that he is not treading the highway of wholeness, or way of holiness, for true thinking and true feeling unite in one Source; and thus, should one truly feel the Truth, he is likewise in possession also of true thinking and knowing.

Indeed, the Love which is God is also the Mind which is God, for how could one exist without the other? Hitherto one may have thought and spoken of them as though they were two distinct qualities, looking to Mind for intelligence and to Love for its feeling. Yet Love is Mind, and Mind is Love, and as we truly possess one, we truly possess the other also.

Should we find that we seem to have the one but not the other, then we are mistaken and have neither, because Love-Wisdom is the eternal I AM, forever delivering revelation and loving understanding to all who are consciously aware of and receptive to It.

Because the spiritual, real man is actually always one with God, he inherits sovereign power to think and act rightly. When it is stated that the spiritual, real man cannot sin, make a mistake, sleep or dream, this is correct: he cannot and does not, since the Self-revealing Light discloses this word "real" to mean precisely a certain state of being—the *perfect* state of God's man.

God's man, consciously aware of and manifesting his true, original, ever-existent state, is rightly termed, "the real man"—meaning, *man functioning in that perfect state.* Of course, this man cannot, and so never does sin, sleep, or err.

It should always be spiritually perceived, however, and consistently maintained, that there is always but the one man to talk about—God's man, and that there never is or could be another. Moreover, every one of us right now is God's man even though we entertained the belief (as did the rich man's son) that we would like to take independent possessions outside the Father's house or state of reality. But even so, this does not change us from being who we are, for it is still certain, "*Now* are we the sons of God."

This explains again why the practitioner says to man called "mortal:" "You are God's spiritual man," for such is the truth. That which is termed mortality is not a reality but an appearance only, and there is before the practitioner a child of God appearing in a dream of separation from his real estate.

When through the revelation of his spiritual insight, one sees this arresting idea, he will then have an intelligent understanding which he can use correctly when speaking of the real man in contrast to the mortal-appearing man. He now knows that there is ever but the one man in different states of awareness.

The state of Reality, which is *the Christ,* is one with God, and it *is* God in that state of perfect expression, the same as the light of the sun is the sun in the state of light. God and Christ are one; that is, God is the invisible, perfect Being—Life, Truth, Love—and Christ, the visible perfect expression, who is "the image of the invisible God." Paul explains specifically: "Now ye are the body of Christ, and members in particular ... so we, being many, are one body in Christ, and every one members one of another." Thus, a Christ-Man could be none other than a particular member of the Christ-Body, acting in the conscious awareness of his original and ever-existing pristine perfection. This is the perfect state which Jesus so gloriously illustrated.

It is of the utmost importance to us, while experiencing, apparently, a false or untrue state (as we all are doing) to know and declare the absolute truth about ourselves *in the Christ,* for by so doing we help to waken ourselves from the mental sleep. And well may we think and say with the great Paul, "As the truth of Christ is in me, no man shall stop me of this boasting ... yet not I, but Christ liveth in me."

The spiritual self and form of you and of me both remain so, for how could God's man ever change his being? He may, however, choose to entertain *a false sense,* as the Bible states, else why did Jesus come to our rescue? Or why did the Self-revealing Light show Isaiah that, "All we like sheep have gone astray: we have turned every one to his own way"? Jesus, knowing this to be the case, elucidated it, and his great love for us, even his supreme sacrifice, prompted him to show us how we might be delivered from such bondage. "Greater love hath no man than this, that a man lay down his life for his friends."

"He came unto his own, and his own received him not" (John 1:11). Jesus came to you and to me, and to all God's children who had become self-estranged from Him. Many were not ready then (nor are so now) to receive the blessed truth of their God-Being and so return to their primal state of perfection. It was with absolute knowledge of the one true Being that Jesus was able to perform his many healings. For instance, seeing the impotence of the self-imposed state of materiality and its claim of disease, he commanded the man with the withered hand to act, then and there, in his true and real state of Being, when he said, "Stretch forth thine hand. And he stretched it out: and his hand was restored whole as the other." The man's obedience repaid him well, did it not? And so in all Jesus' miracles he furnished the disproof of sin and evil by destroying sickness and limitations to the sense and sight of all.

Dear reader, does not this clear explanation of life convince you that it is true and right? Surely, you must now see more clearly than ever before that "Greater is he (the Christ state of man) that is in you than he (the mortal-appearing state of man) that is in the world." You must now see clearly that your perfect Self and perfect form *both* exist in the here and now, despite any contrary appearance, intact and within you, outside any dream or false belief, exactly as both the self of your waking state and its form exist here in this world, intact, though in your sleep and dream you appear to take on another state and another form; in other words, the self and form of the sleeper undergo no change whatsoever, and are unaffected by any dream.

Thus you should be able now to willingly let go all thinking and speaking of yourself and others as "mortals" for, indeed, this is the state which you should gladly lose sight of so as to again function in the true and real state of perfection and immortality. For how could you ever hope to make manifest the immortal state while you persistently speak of yourself and others as "mortals"? "Where there is no (whole) vision (of perfection), the people perish: but he that keepeth the (spiritual) law (of Jesus Christ), happy is he" (Prov. 29:18).

It is by seeing this reassuring fact that you may also perceive clearly just where the healing should take place—namely, *in one's own sense and awareness, in his vision, thought, feeling and action.* Should one attempt to bring changes directly to the body or conditions, he would do this in his sleep, or self-imposed state: for it is obvious that were he awake and alive to the fact that he is ever the perfect man, instead of a human being, he would perceive that his harmony lay solely in his return in awareness to the real state of himself.

Spiritual healing, therefore, has really nothing directly to do with changing discordant physical conditions, but deals only with God's man who entertains a false belief, the *very* man Jesus meant when he said, "For the Son of man is come to seek and to save that which was lost." Spiritual healing takes place by showing one who he is, whence he came, and whither he goeth. Thus one must intensely yearn and resolutely aim for that state which is rightfully his, and so make the supreme effort to return to it.

Jesus recognized and acknowledged only one man, God's man, but he was always aware of his two-fold position, namely, when he functioned in his real and true state as the perfect Son of God, and on the other hand, when he voluntarily imposed upon himself a dream of separation from this true state and was called the son of man. Jesus came to disillusion such a man and so restore to him his true state of being.

"When that which is perfect is come, then that which is in part shall be done away." As this clearer light breaks in upon us, and remains to bless us, surely our mistaken beliefs about ourselves and of others as ever being "mortals" will fade away, for no darkness can remain in the presence of the Light. When you actually see with inner spiritual vision that the real Self of you ever exists within you, and that the discordant human appearance is an unreality depending wholly upon your own state of awareness, then surely you will cease forever to allude to yourself as a mortal and will insist upon thinking and speaking of yourself *always* and *only as* the spiritual man of God.

Also you will see how true it is that as your accompanying form expresses your inner state of awareness, it is your *reflection* always. Our life, our being, and our true consciousness certainly are *not* reflections of God, for all the life there is, all the being there is, and all the true consciousness there is, are identical with the one all-inclusive God-Being—the I AM THAT I AM. There is none besides Him. When it is said that "man is the reflection of

God," what this should be seen to mean is that all true *man*ifestation is the reflection of God. That is, the body of Christ is truly the reflection of God, Spirit, as Paul perceived and stated, just the very same as the light of the sun is the reflection of the sun. They are a unit. So man, fully aware of and functioning in that true state, which is the Christ, is a "member in particular" of that Light-Body and shares in expressing "the fullness of the Godhead bodily."

Love-Wisdom alone can and will save us. Our intense love for God, and for our perfect real Self, and our intense yearning to become consciously aware of the truth of being, will surely prepare us all for the full awakening. Truly we find Wisdom only in being Love. When we say with all sincere and earnest aspiration, "I will arise and go unto Love," then we are starting out, at last, toward our true home and our divine reality.

The change of circumstances and conditions which you feel should take place from discord to harmony, from war to peace, from limitation to abundance, shall surely come to pass, even as you well know in your heart that it must, but the manner of it will not be that of labored thinking nor of strife, but shall be a transfiguration which shall come about naturally and effortlessly as you believe in and accept your real Christ state. Here, in this reinstatement, you are heir to the very things for which you so earnestly longed in your dream of separation from them; here, too, you may experience the truth of your claim, "All that the Father hath is mine."

Were there any other way I would have told you, said the all-loving Master. There can be nothing save that which *is*, and thus there is no way out of a dream except by waking from it; nothing can make a dream over into reality. Is this not so? Regardless even of the beauty, love and harmony which you may see expressed in your dream, in the end you will find that it had no substance in it whatever, except such as you assume to give it.

Now, to make our return from a state of mental darkness back to the full light of reality is by no means as easy as turning on the electric switch at our elbow, but great demands are made upon us. The more we can see, however, that we are not required to step from one place to another, nor from one condition to another, but only from one state of awareness to another, the sooner the awakening comes.

"As in Adam all die, even so in Christ shall all be made alive." As in the state of believing we are John or Mary Jones, we shall go through the experience of passing from one plane to another — though still remaining in the dream — so in functioning in the Christ state of Being, ever one with the Father, (hence ever Spirit, Life, Truth,

Love,) we shall all be made awake and know even as each is known of the Father-God.

"Whosoever believeth that Jesus is the Christ is born of God." Whoever sees and accepts, claims and endeavors to function in the Christ state which Jesus embodied, realizes that he is receiving the light of God. If we cannot understand this Christ state through the life and teaching of Jesus, then how else will we ever be able to come into a knowledge of it?

Your original mistake was in belief only. Thus it is that your own Christ-Self shall redeem you as you function in that Christ state. This state does not await you in some other place or time, but is as close to you now as ever it could be; so recognize it as with you, in you—*you*—and verily you will find it so to be.

You do not need to leave your place of sleep in order to express the Self of your waking state; in fact, if you believed this to be so, you would still be sleeping! The waking state in no way depends upon the sleep, but only upon you, the sleeper. Even to remain in the pleasant dreams we sometimes have would deprive you of the still more abundant life experiences of the waking state. How else, dear reader, can we ever hope to see and feel the things as they really are except by thinking, seeing, feeling, acting and being in our true state? For only to the Son in his Father's house does He say, "Son, thou art ever with me, and all that I have is thine."

In the Christ state you are sinless: "In him is no sin ... without spot or blemish ... neither guile in his mouth." In the Christ state you experience no darkness: "He that followeth me shall not walk in darkness, but shall have the light of life. I am the light of the world."

In the Christ state you have all abundance: "All things whatsoever the Father hath are mine." In the Christ state you shall live without death: "I am the resurrection and the life. Whosoever liveth and believeth on me shall never die." In the Christ state the glory of Truth is ever revealing Itself to you: "All things that I have heard of my Father, I have made known unto you ... The things which God hath prepared for them which love him, God hath revealed (them) unto us by his Spirit." In the Christ state you enjoy understanding and inspiration: "I am the truth ... In whom are hid all the treasures of wisdom and knowledge ... Christ shall give thee light."

In the Christ state you have all power: "All power is given unto me in heaven and in earth ... I give unto you power over all the power of the enemy: and nothing shall by any means hurt you." In the Christ state you experience a perfect body: "Your body is the temple of the Holy Ghost ... In him (the Christ) dwelleth all the fullness of the Godhead bodily."

The Christ state alone is our Redeemer, Saviour, Deliverer, Lord and Righteousness. "Ye are Christ's and Christ is God's ... He is the first-born of every creature ... Ye are complete in him ... Christ is in all."

Then what could be the meaning of the "second coming of Christ" but that we are to take those steps which will enable us to function in the Christ state and so see him as he is? Our first concept of Jesus may have been of some God-man who would vicariously save us from evil in ourselves and translate us from earth to heaven; or we may have taken him as an example to follow, so that we might thereby be able to overcome the seeming evil conditions as he did and so ultimately reach harmony.

Through the transparency of the Self-revealing Light, we shall behold him from the mount of vision, and so seek only to accept him as our *very being*: "That they may be made perfect in one." This is his "second coming" to us.

The spiritual, real man is, of course, perfect at all times. He cannot and does not sin, mistake or err. He is without birth, age, death or impurity of any kind. He is as perfect as the Father in heaven is perfect, since he is a member of that infinitely perfect state of God-Being called *the Christ.*

What we all desire to know more fully is how we may again be an *active* member in this Christ state of being—the state of perfection which we had with the Father before the world (of evil) was. Jesus himself gave the perfect answer with and by his own life. When the repentant ones came to Jesus and he restored them to health and harmony, was he not, then and there, dramatizing the "Father" whom he said in the parable came to meet the wayward and penitent one? Did he not pointedly say, "I am come in my Father's name"? We find, too, in the prophecy of Zacharias the following: "Blessed be the Lord God of Israel; *for he hath visited and redeemed his people.*" In this same sense, Jesus was "the everlasting Father."

When man deflected from his original state and form of perfection, he found himself in a state and form of imperfection, wherein he called everything by other names, for it is written in Genesis, "And whatsoever Adam called every living creature, that was the name thereof." But do not mistake, dear reader, it was not the Christ-Man who became a material or human being; never allow such an idea to be entertained by you. Light must ever be light and can never be darkness.

When we withdraw ourselves from that perfect Christ state, we find ourselves in a state where sin, sickness and limitation of all kinds are seen about us. The conceiver of the "Adam dream" was not and never could be the Christ-Man, but was and is *anyone who does not choose to remain in that very position.* When we remain awake, we are incapable of experiencing night dreams, but when we choose to "go to sleep" then we enter another state which is far removed from our waking experience. Precisely in the same way, when we remained in the Christ state and functioned as the Christ man, we knew no sin. But when we chose darkness rather than light, we automatically entered another so-called state which has since been termed "the Adam dream"; and this is precisely the "far country" referred to in Jesus' parable of the prodigal son.

It is when man *deflects* from the Christ state of knowing and being the Christ-Man that he entertains false beliefs of his identity, and of everything else as well; and thus it was this same viewpoint which led to the conviction and consequent statement that mortals are the Adam dreamers. Now let us examine into this further. To begin with, a "mortal" is *not* a man, inasmuch as no other but God can create man, and so man must ever be *immortal*.

Who or what, then, is a "mortal?" This word implies primarily *a false mental state*, which we all entered when we turned away from the Father's house—our true Christ state of being. In this *assumed* state men are seen as "mortals," but in the Self-revealing Light we know, as did Jesus, that man is immortal *always*. Thus it is not "mortals" but we, the children of God, who are the Adam dreamers; and we are the very ones who must put off a dream state and a dream man, and put on the real state and real man.

According to the Bible, Adam was the name given to the first sinful appearing man, the first man to deflect from his original state of perfection. Later on, Luke, in tracing the genealogy of Jesus back to the original first man makes this arresting and enlightening statement: "Adam was the son of God" (Luke 3:38).

Probably most of you have never before thought of Adam in this light, but now it may be really seen and understood that this is so. And seeing how this is true of Adam, we shall also see how it is likewise true of every one of us, which makes this subject a practical and paramount point for clarification, enabling us to proceed in the unraveling of that baffling and age-long problem of human existence.

The question to now answer is: How could Adam be the son of God and yet appear as a sinful human being? First, the Garden of Eden symbolizes paradise, perfection, the same as "the father's house" in Jesus' parable. Adam, the son of God, identical with the rich man's son, strangely enough, was not satisfied with perfection, for we find Adam symbolically portrayed as indulging in forbidden fruit (leaving the perfect state) the same as did the rich man's son when he attempted to personalize his spiritual possessions. Both these instances lay bare the "original sin," and so preclude the possibility of tracing the cause of evil back any further than these steps just indicated.

As elaborately set forth in the pages of this Series, the perfect man must be seen and known as a Son of God acting in the perfect Christ state; and the "limited human being" should be seen and known as the state and form the same son *assumed* when he renounced his original heavenly estate of being. Now, as we all must see, such an assumed position of imperfection is, of course, *a false state*, and necessarily, then, it is temporal; and thus it will vanish as man reverses himself—forsakes the earthy for the heavenly, as Paul so aptly puts it:

> *Behold, I show you a mystery; We shall not all (always) sleep (continue in the false state), but we shall all be changed (back to our original position of perfection) ... then shall be brought to pass the saying that is written, Death is swallowed up in victory.*

Thus we see clearly and understand fully the words which came to Isaiah in his vision, while sighting Jesus the Christ as our deliverer, when he said:

> *To give knowledge of salvation unto his people by the remission of their sins ... whereby the dayspring from on high hath visited us ... to give light to them that sit in darkness and in the*

*shadow of death, to guide our feet into the way
of peace.*

Verily, the "altogether lovely" Christ Jesus is
the one ever perfect Son of God who set before us
"an open door and no man can shut it."

This new and inspiring vision now opens our
understanding to grasp more clearly than ever
before the inspired word of God from Genesis to
Revelation. Each of the prophets knew and wrote
about the history of the sons and daughters of God
from the very beginning; and with what feeling
then of mingled sorrow and joy, shame and glory
we now read again those profound and deeply
stirring words of the prophet, Isaiah:

*He was wounded for our transgressions, he
was bruised for our iniquities: the chastisement
of our peace is upon him; and with his stripes
we are healed.*

In very truth, then, we should ever keep the
name *Jesus* as "above every name that is named,"
for we now see, doubtless as never before, just
why it was necessary that Jesus should come into
the world — that we might know who we are,
whence we came, whither we go, and how we
may be redeemed from our assumed state and
again partake fully of our heavenly peace and
glory.

Surely there is no greater joy than to become acquainted with the *Self* as the Self-revealing Light. Then we can truly say with the apostle, "He that abideth in the doctrine of Christ, he hath both the Father (Life) and the Son (Expression)" for the Father "hath given all things" to man in his true estate as the Son-Self.

Every one of us may now be God's law of Life and Love unto himself, and so perceive clearly the great necessity that we recognize and obey Jesus' command, "Neither be ye (in your earthly state) called masters: for one (state) is your Master, even Christ." Each of us who is willing to accept this indwelling Christ-Self as our Master will also be willing to accept the gracious invitation ever waiting us each, "Behold, I stand at the door and knock; if any man hear my voice and open the door, I will come in to him." And when we open the door to that Self—our Master—we open to the power given spiritual man from the beginning.

Reading the Scriptures from a theological point of view, one is taught to believe that Jesus was God in person, coming in the form of mortal man to deliver from sin anyone who would believe and accept Him and His vicarious atonement. Reading the Scriptures from another viewpoint, one believes that Jesus Christ was not God in person, but the very best man ever to be on earth, demonstrating for himself, as well as for all who would follow his teaching, how to overcome, as he did, "the world, the flesh and the devil." This view presents Jesus as the "wayshower" and does not include the doctrine of the vicarious atonement, but that of individual progress and demonstration out of the flesh or mortality into the "glorious liberty of the sons of God," by way of spiritual evolution.

But there is a still higher view of Jesus Christ and of his life and teaching on earth, which is this: Jesus was the Christ-Man because he was the Son of God who lived in the Christ state. Thus, being ever one with the Father, he was Life, Truth and Love; and he never lost sight of this nor forgot it. He knew the end (perfection) from the beginning (perfection). This is why he said, "Father, glorify me with thine own self, with the glory which I had with thee before the world was." Also he said, "I came from the Father and I return to the Father." Moreover, he knew what was true about him was likewise true of every one of us—"that they may be perfect in one."

Jesus appeared in the same mortal or human form as we do, otherwise he would not have so well understood our present state of mental sleep. He healed men of all kinds of sickness, of sin and of death. How did he do it? Through his inner knowledge of himself, and themselves, as actually the I-Am-Self, "the only begotten of the Father," and through his spiritual awareness of his own, and their own, original and ever-existing state of perfection—the *Christ of God.* He was the Christ and announced himself as such. He was God in nature, essence and being, and he loved and lived this verity.

Jesus insistently declared, "Without me ye can do nothing;" that is, unless you see me as verily the Christ-Man, ever one with the Father, you cannot discern yourselves to be fashioned in the selfsame likeness. It is impossible for you to awake and so resume your original perfect state as consciously one with the Father in any way other than by accepting Me—the Christ-Self—to be *your* Self also. With this same perception Paul said, "He that acknowledgeth the Son (to be the Christ-Man) hath (automatically) the Father also."

Jesus was the Love-Way unto himself, the Love-Light on his own path, and the very Love-Truth which he so perfectly manifested. And so, too, must we all be.

Love is the within and the without of us all and of all manifested things, for Love permeates and pervades all existence. "Love envieth not; is not puffed up. Love never faileth." But whether there be mental misconceptions, they shall fail; whether there be abstract statements of Truth, they shall cease; whether there be personal knowledge, it too, shall utterly vanish away.

When perfect Love is come and abides, then that which is not perfect Love shall be done away. Without this perfect Love, existence were barren and empty; for Love is the very substance of Being, the Alpha and Omega of our search to know our own perfection and to find our own Self-harmony.

Our very being is Love-Being. Our very life is Love-Life. Our very substance is Love-Substance. Love is the All-inclusive, and forever, the I AM THAT I AM. When all methods of thinking and all ways of stating the truth have failed you, then bring yourself into an at-one-ment with the presence of that Love which never faileth, for love in the heart will lift up the fainting, give peace and comfort to the sorrowing, and bless the weary seeker of Truth with surcease from pain, weakness, fear and trouble, by Its all-freeing presence.

Let your love be gentle and kind, compassionate and understanding, and it will deliver and heal you even though all other ways have failed. This love, truly felt and expressed in the everyday living, dries the eyes of tears, stills the troubled sense, and never fails to satisfy the heart's desire for all the gifts of the Spirit.

Love in me blesses, lifts up, inspires. Love in me illumines, enriches, satisfies. Love in me giveth all, for Love *is* all, and hath all to give; thus, " He that dwelleth in love dwelleth in God, and God in him." Love is my real and genuine treasure, verily the pearl of great price, for my Love-Self supplies me with life, everlasting; with harmony, never-changing; and with good, without measure.

Where is this great Love which never fails to satisfy our every longing? Dear reader, It is to be found right within you and me: *for this Love is here exactly where we are.* As I imbibe and partake of It, as I feel and embody It, as I really love divinely and unselfishly, tenderly and compassionately, I am then at-one with the Love which is God.

As I let Love possess me, as I let Love permeate and entirely fill me, as I let Love become the supreme reality to me—that is, even life itself— then I am indeed one with Love, and then does Love completely satisfy my every need.

For Love is God. Hence, as I entertain Love in my heart, I am actually aware of His presence. This, then, is the *atonement,* my atonement with Love, my real Being—my putting off the old man with dreams of separation, and putting on the awakened state of my pure and pristine Being.

As I recognize Love and Reality to be one, then shall I understand that my health is in and of Love, and so it is Reality, unchangeable; my happiness is in and of Love, and so it is Reality, unalterable; my wealth is in and of Love, and so it is Reality, indestructible. My health, happiness and wealth all abide in and of Love; therefore as I put on, or literally become Love, I simultaneously regain my primal spiritual stature, "of the fullness of Christ."

I shall fear no evil, for Love is with me. Love opens my way into green pastures; Love unlocks for me the prison door. Love is my safety and security, always. Love multiplies my supply of good to any proportion needful. Love reveals to me the necessary thoughts or things, close at hand, which before seemed far from me.

Love is the One "altogether lovely," helping me to forgive without question, for whosoever dwelleth in Love dwelleth in the all-good, and the all-good in him. Love is supreme and o'er all victorious. Love withholdeth no good thing from me. Love giveth to me the right to choose Love for myself, for in giving all to me, Love requires all of me. Love requires my heart's fervent devotion, my heart's full homage and praise.

Love in my heart imparts purity, wholeness, bliss. Love in my heart imparts inspiration, illumination, faith and revelation. By Its own presence, Love in me cancels my false sense of lack and limitation; and by Its own presence, Love in me shall free me from the dream of separation from my true Selfhood—the Christ—and so deliver me from all evil.

Love is the universal language. Love is the "lost" word. Love is the Alpha and Omega, the forever I AM THAT I AM. But in order that Love become *my* language, *my* Deliverer and *my* Reality of all-good, here and now, I must take Love into my heart and serve Love with all my strength and being. I must make Love the supreme Reality in my life. I must worship and adore Love fervently and with intensity of being. And I must aim to become Love. For when I have become Love to myself, then the darkness is as light before me, the dream is gone, and I am conscious of Reality only.

So it is possible for man to be healed at this moment of any false sense of lack, sickness or limitation, *by dwelling in Love,* even as Jesus taught and so marvelously illustrated. Moses, once glimpsing this simple yet stupendous fact, exclaimed, "What doth the Lord thy God require of thee but to love him, and to serve the Lord thy God with all thy heart and with all thy soul."

In this love within man's own heart lies his complete dominion, his wisdom, power and glory—yea, his life, eternal.

In the "beginning" there were allotted to man six days in which to dispel the darkness which he himself created by turning from the awareness that in his Father's house abideth the infinite, all-satisfying Love. It is written: "Six days shalt thou labor to do all thy work" (Ex. 2:9). And we are told by the discerning Peter that "one day is as a thousand years." Inasmuch, therefore, as four thousand years elapsed from the dating of Bible history to the advent of Jesus on earth, obviously the sixth day will close with the year 1999.

Then comes the *seventh* day—the day of rest, or the millennium. Today, nearly two thousand years since that great influx of spiritual light and illumination delivered to mankind in the person and teaching of Jesus, the Christ, we find our full restoration to our Father's house, (the true estate of being) close at hand. Particularly during these past fifty years, more and more of that wondrous story of Jesus' life and teaching on earth has entered deep into the heart of man, and so taken root. Now, great multitudes are reaching out toward that good which is theirs by divine right.

The four thousand years prior to Jesus' time were given over almost entirely to attaining wisdom, which is recognized as the masculine element of Consciousness—woman being considered of lower rank and lesser intelligence. Then, however, came a woman—the Virgin Mary—who gave forth a great light, even the light of the world, illustrating love, (the feminine element) as encompassing wisdom (the masculine element). Since that time until now, woman has slowly but steadily risen to the height where she now stands.

Today, woman rightfully enlists and compels the attention of the world, for she has climbed to reach the side of man in nearly every endeavor; and she is destined to fully succeed in this century—to reach her goal and so complete her work, even as man has done before her. Before the close of these six working days, great and mighty events are to come to pass. We shall see woman standing beside man, his rightful mate and equal: for so she was created.

Woman's day typifies the *fullness* of Love—
that state of consciousness which ends wars,
cancels misunderstandings, transcends fears and
limitations, scales the heights and reaches the
mount of God where perfection stands revealed—
and behold, all is light. This Horeb-height is the
zenith of demonstration, for here Truth and Love,
Man and Woman are seen as *one*, not two, and a
new state of living begins.

When the "mist" or misconception of Life and
Being first appeared in man's thought and vision,
it included among other falsities, the belief that the
masculine and feminine elements of Consciousness, called man and woman, were two separate
states and entities, instead of *one unit of Consciousness,* wherein and whereof Wisdom and Love
combine and operate as one.

In the Self-revealing Light, man and woman
complement each other and so constitute units of
Consciousness. When the son of God chose to
separate himself from the awareness of perfection
as ever abiding within him and desired to make
such possession personal, he then found himself
believing that he was separated from part of
himself; and so, down the ages, (in the dream)
both man and woman have ever been seeking the
real mate.

Now, when it is clearly and spiritually revealed to the individual that Mind (the positive element) and Love (the negative element) are not,

and never have been, two separate entities, each operating distinctly, but ever have been and forever shall be one identical Being, one Love-Mind, then it is clearly seen that a true marriage in this world symbolizes the perpetual and ever-existing oneness of Man and Woman in Reality.

Such light discloses each spiritual man to be a unit of knowing and feeling characteristics; that is, a man and a woman, divinely united, represent *one* spiritual man. They are "joined" without any marriage ceremony, even as Jesus intimated, for they are joined spiritually, in heaven, reality, and will ever so remain.

This explains why there has been, and continues to be, great upheaval in so-called married life on earth, as so often marriage is not a union of two already divinely united ones, and frequently, then, they separate in what is termed "divorce."

For each woman there is her divine mate, and similarly, of course, for each man. When they have found each other (as must eventually take place) they will be one unit of Consciousness, *one spiritual man*—the male representing wisdom, intelligence and understanding, and the female representing love, light and power; two distinct individuals operating so perfectly together to be as one in thought and feeling, though each, of course, expressing a body or form of his or her own.

In order that this marvelous and striking revelation becomes more universally seen and experienced, one should start with the premise that though mind, understanding, wisdom or intelligence represents the masculine element of Spirit, Life, and though love, light, revelation and power represents the feminine element, they are never to be thought of as though they were *two* entities, distinct one from the other, but must always be seen as one inseparable Being, one Love-Wisdom which forever remains the I AM THAT I AM.

This explains more clearly why it is so necessary that each of us should *understand* and *love* the Truth, for attempting to accept Truth intellecttually, or without love, deprives one of the light; and moreover, as it was the Virgin Mary (woman) who gave birth to Jesus (man) so it must be that *only* through love will true understanding ever become fully known.

The feminine element of Life is the higher and so encompasses the masculine, as perfectly illustrated by Mary and Jesus. Thus, the way of absolute understanding is through Love, and Love alone.

Following this illumination one will naturally see that there is for each the perfect mate, even from the very "beginning." And so the acceptance of such revelation will help to make the necessary true recognition possible; thus many heartaches and much dissatisfaction will then be avoided.

However, even though it is known by two certain wedded individuals on earth that the perfect union has not been represented, nevertheless, wherever possible, such marriage should continue, and each should do his or her part in maintaining the peace and harmony so essential for individual and conjugal happiness.

Let each one act and feel (even under sometimes trying circumstances) as "one" and not two, and so a finer and richer experience of the all-good will inevitably take place.

In this world no one need feel that another one deprives him of any particular good, nor that he may be a channel obstructing the good of any. Such is never a fact. As the light and heat of the sun are available to us all alike, and as this sun supplies us individually so that none of us need feel a personal responsibility in sharing his sunlight with another, so in this world, we should know that each of us receives his supply of health, wealth and happiness from God, the great powerhouse of all-good; hence, we should never feel that we can deprive another in any way of the constant flow of the infinite good to him.

One should ever be translating his vision from that of a material sense of good or supply to that of the spiritual; then he will perceive that man is always being supplied richly with every good there is, since to everyone, everywhere, God supplies every good and perfect thing.

Thus if one is called upon to give spiritual help to another, he should first of all perceive and understand just *who* this individual really is, whence he came and whither he goeth. Then he will know for a certainty his changeless and ever-continuous perfection and wholeness in every way, and the groundless occasion for any fear.

Holding steadfastly to the absolute facts of Being, he will be able also to clearly perceive the nothingness or unreality of the apparent contrary evidence. And love in his heart will be the light which will cause any darkness to vanish.

Jesus cast out devils and spoke with authority. He could do this because he knew perfectly that any wrong education was powerless in itself, and that all false beliefs relating to the events of a far country were unreal because untrue. He cast them out without conceding any consideration whatever to them, and so proved beyond a shadow of doubt the absolute truth that our genuine Being is intact and present always, even though, as in the case of Lazarus, the belief in death had been present for several days.

To Jesus, the perfect One, all things lay revealed, and thus it was to us he said,

He that believeth on me, the works that I do shall he do also. And these signs shall follow them that believe; in my name they shall cast out devils; they shall speak with new tongues;

they shall take up serpents and if they drink any deadly thing it shall not hurt them; they shall lay hands on the sick and they shall recover.

"Ye shall know the truth and the truth shall make you free," he proclaims to every one of us. What man is it who shall know this truth? Surely, it could be none other than God's man! For "He (Jesus) shall save his people from their sins ... He came to seek and to find that which was lost."

Ever the eternal promise reads: "Though your sins be as scarlet, they shall be white as snow; though they be red like crimson, they shall be as wool." No matter the nature of the dream nor the seeming time it may have consumed, nothing can change us from being who and what we are — sons and daughters of God, and joint-heirs with Jesus in the Christ, who "is all, and in all."

Thus, walking in the Self-revealing Light we are all waking in our Father's house, even as Jesus promised — to find ourselves children of the day, expressing the perfect, original spiritual man.